Viva Studymates

Growing Workplace Champions

Viva Studymates

Growing Workplace Champions

How to develop coaching and mentoring within an organisation

Chris Sangster

Viva Books

New Delhi | Mumbai | Chennai | Kolkata | Bangalore | Hyderabad | Kochi | Guwahati

First Indian Edition 2010

VIVA BOOKS PRIVATE LIMITED

- 4737/23 Ansari Road, Daryaganj, New Delhi 110 002
  E-mail: vivadelhi@vivagroupindia.net, Tel. 42242200
- 76, Service Industries, Shirvane, Sector 1, Nerul, Navi Mumbai 400 706
  E-mail: vivamumbai@vivagroupindia.net, Tel. 27721273, 27721274
- Jamals Fazal Chambers, 26 Greams Road, Chennai 600 006
  E-mail: vivachennai@vivagroupindia.net, Tel. 28290304, 28294241
- B-103, Jindal Towers, 21/1A/3 Darga Road, Kolkata 700 017
  E-mail: vivakolkata@vivagroupindia.net, Tel. 22836381, 22816713
- 7, Sovereign Park Apartments, 56-58, K. R. Road, Basavanagudi, Bangalore 560 004
  E-mail: vivabangalore@vivagroupindia.net, Tel. 26607409, 26607410
- 101-102 Mughal Marc Apartments, 3-4-637 to 641, Narayanguda, Hyderabad 500 029
  E-mail: vivahyderabad@vivagroupindia.net, Tel. 27564481, 27564482
- Beevi Towers, First Floor, SRM Road, Kaloor, Kochi 682 018, Kerala
  E-mail: vivakochi@vivagroupindia.net, Tel: 0484-2403055, 2403056
- 232, GNB Road, Beside UCO Bank, Silpukhuri, Guwahati 781 003
  E-mail: vivaguwahati@vivagroupindia.net, Tel: 0361-2666386

www.vivagroupindia.com

Published by arrangement with
Studymates Limited
PO Box 2, Bishops Lydeard,
Somerset TA4 3YE,
United Kingdom

ISBN : 978-81-309-1305-6

Published by Vinod Vasishtha for Viva Books Private Limited, 4737/23, Ansari Road, Daryaganj, New Delhi-110 002. Printed and bound by Swan Press, New Delhi.

M0000 / M0400

Contents

Foreword

It is a great pleasure to have been asked to write a foreword for this new book by Chris Sangster, whom I have known for many years. His premise is that anyone and everyone can become a Champion in the work place. I absolutely believe this to be true. If given the opportunity and if people empower themselves, then magic can be created.

A shift perhaps has to take place within the thinking of management and workers to believe that there is a spark of greatness in everyone. It may be that some have more empathy than others or that some may have greater capacity for strategic thinking or new ideas. Whatever that individual spark is, its development can contribute to the overall effect. What a difference it would make if all involved held the holistic view set out in Chris's model, of the inter-relatedness of an organisation – and believed that everyone can make a difference in this way. That in itself is an empowering idea.

Chris stresses the importance of teams recognising and working towards co-operation. My experience is that the majority of work and sports teams currently spend around ninety percent of their time in the assertion phase. If they can recognise this and choose to collaborate more, then both results and relationships can be positively transformed. The decision has to be theirs, agreeing and acting upon a common inspiring vision and/or mission.

Another aspect which Chris stresses is the benefit of learner and workplace champion relationships being in close proximity, aiding consolidation and on-going problem solving. I would add that the solution may often be as simple as converting statements into questions, in order to empower the learner further.

Like Chris, I have spent many years helping managers to enhance their communication skills, adding to their ability to give advice. If done well, this improved skill can provide the step change required in corporate development. There is no reason why this coaching/mentoring should be limited to managers. As "workplace champions", everyone has a different perspective and expertise to contribute and Chris directs his experience in further education and business training towards implementing this full range of competency development.

I commend this as a thought provoking read and would hope that the essence of the encapsulated intent is discovered by the reader. As co-creators of our world, what can be better than to involve ourselves in the creation of our own ideal environment.

David Hemery CBE
Vice Chairman, British Olympic Association
Chairman, Confederation of British Sport
Director, Developing Potential Ltd

1 Growing Workplace Champions

One-minute overview

This chapter establishes what we mean by the "workplace champion" – and how this compares with the traditional definitions for mentoring and coaching. It sets the scene for our model, working towards involving widespread championing within an organisation and looks at how this fits into the overall learning and development plans for an organisation.

1. Introduction

Imagine a workplace where skills and knowledge are exchanged freely, allowing any individual to overcome those blocks which may be preventing them from doing their job competently. Picture a workplace where most, if not all, of those working there have the skills necessary to transfer this information to others in an ordered way – and are happy to do so. Imagine the speed of response and the time saving involved – and consider the cost savings to the company. Think of the benefits that such a system will bring to individuals' development, team interactions and departmental co-operation. The good news is that such an integrated system already exists … and it's called Workplace Championing. This book will show you how it works.

Remember – our development path here is not heading towards training workplace champions to be accredited trainers. The model is focused on developing people who can (and wish to) pass information and skills to others. Developing workplace champions involves finding ways of building on this natural enthusiasm, to give them structures and support which will make their involvement as easy as possible.

Where do we stand?

We are becoming a nation – a world – of individual thinkers. Individual – and more independent – while at the same time embracing notions of interdependency. With the internet and an empowered attitude towards identifying what we want, most people are also in a better position to ensure that they achieve it. And, in the worlds of information and skills competency, we're a lot clearer about specifically what it is individuals need to know in order to progress in their chosen directions. "Bite sized learning" is a highly popular form of learning – why attend a two-day public course if the specific information and practice you require can be achieved in two hours? Why consider generalised information when work-specific solutions are on your doorstep? Why settle for second best when you can become a workplace champion?

What is a Workplace Champion?

A workplace champion is someone who possesses a particular skill and/or area of knowledge, which s/he is competent at applying, and is willing to pass on to someone else who is lacking some or all of this information. This champion may require assistance at first, at a structured though fairly informal level, to encourage successful involvement in the process. While this involvement is likely to start small it is also likely to grow in line with confidence, support and motivation.

Expand this championing potential throughout the workplace or organisation and you have a vast scope for "bite-sized", tailored inputs of information. This has the benefits of being provided on site, as well as being available flexibly on demand. This allows championing to respond to the majority of learning and development needs in existence within the organisation. Everyone can potentially give and receive information through this championing model – all that's necessary is the right level of preparation and support, coupled with a consistent reinforcement from management.

Transferring Learning between people

So, welcome to the world of the workplace champion – where information and skills can be exchanged co-operatively. Welcome to the initiative to encourage everyone to become involved in this transfer of learning, applying a range of simple techniques. Join in the efforts to get these messages across effectively.

A key driver for this way of thinking is the belief that, overall, we can receive assistance from the system in the same way that we can provide input to it – so there's potentially something in it for all of us. Assuming that you invest time in helping someone else to get over a hurdle, you could expect some reciprocal assistance yourself when your own block to progression appears.

The Correct foundations – confident competency

The system (only) works if:

- the attitude's right and
- a support structure is in place that motivates and maintains the momentum.

Don't consider becoming involved in implementation, or any associated training, until the infrastructure has been agreed fully and is firmly in place. Without this essential prior planning, the structure will fail, hours of time will be wasted and an enormous opportunity will have been lost.

"Confident competency"

Remember that phrase … it's what the system being advocated here is all about. Just think how you've probably learned your present skills – for example, those techniques you use on the computer. You may have absorbed many of these techniques not so much by attending full-time courses as through receiving tips and demonstrations from colleagues.

Add to this your own trial and error and some direct e-coaching from the help screens – and you're almost there. All this will have been supported by timely, informal on-job reinforcement from colleagues to get you past periodic blockages.

Bite-size learning

This mix of informal coaching, mentoring and other simple techniques from our workplace champions encourages specific "bite-sized" learning to happen. We're looking for the shortest delay between the time when information is needed and when it is actually delivered. This means we have a working organisation with expertise that is being spread throughout by effective, planned management that means workplace champions are used as a responsive training source when required.

With a growing range of workplace champions in place, the follow-up reinforcement of learning on the job will also be available "on tap", by mutual arrangement. They're likely to be work colleagues, so help literally is at hand. Overcoming over these early learning blockages is a real motivator for all concerned, potentially allowing virtually unhindered progress. It also vastly reduces wasteful downtimes, when activity is arrested by lack of a specific piece of information or knowledge. When working co-operatively, our model provides the keys to unlock these frustrating barriers.

Workplace champion – empowered learner

You can be one of these workplace champions – as well as swapping hats to become an empowered learner at other times. Notice the title: the individual is someone who is empowered or involved in his or her development. As this empowered learner, you'll help to identify the necessary information you need to receive from others. In this mode, they'll be acting as skills and knowledge champions for the particular subject area you need to develop further.

It's a simple, sharing arrangement, out of which workplace co-operation evolves. So – think champion ... think empowerment – think co-operation!

Workplace Champion – a definition

Before we go any further, let's bring these various ideas together in a more formal definition of what we mean by a workplace champion.

A workplace champion is anyone who has a competency level in particular skills and/or knowledge and the capability to pass on specific areas of this information to others. The intended outcome is that the empowered learner's identified shortfall will be resolved and s/he will be able to progress effectively. Championing combines a range of skills and techniques, applied in an informal though structured way.

The Purpose

Throughout this book, we'll be examining an overall championing strategy that can meet the internal development needs of particular teams – and potentially the entire workforce. It'll focus on special applications of mentoring, coaching and related skills within the workplace – but we can equally adapt this championing to operate effectively within more general groupings in our non-work, life situations.

Seeing the broader context

As well as considering the skills and techniques involved in the process, we'll review how wide scale workplace championing fits within a continuing professional development (CPD) plan. Some organisations refer to this as PDP, or a personal development plan. Whatever we call it, think of it as the path built from blending a full range of possible techniques, training courses and applied learning resources. Notice this blend. We're not advocating workplace championing as "the total training solution" – no one technique will meet every requirement totally. Business needs differ, as do the empowered learners involved in the process.

Individuals and their pathway to learning

Each individual is progressing along his or her specific path, achieving identified and necessary development along the way. However, because the learner has been directly involved in the identification and specification of the necessary shortfalls, his/her motivation to learn appropriate information, fill the gaps and achieve outcomes can be expected to be high. A major part of the champion role is to help to maintain this high level of motivation.

A Combination of Skills: Coaching and Mentoring

Let's consider the traditional descriptions, which identify the two key skills and techniques of mentoring and coaching. Championing combines elements of both of these, along with additional techniques including on-the-job training and bite-sized learning. Once we've established these foundations, we can then explore our understanding of what makes the workplace champion really effective.

Learning from sport

You'll probably have seen sports coaching on television. Think of coaching in sports such as swimming, or athletics, or golf – rather than football coaching. This is because we'll be considering coaching and mentoring more as an individual, one-to-one activity, with each person being treated slightly differently and uniquely. Football coaching may give the impression that the players are all being directed by the coach or trainer to perform much the same activity. The approach used in football could perhaps be defined more as training than coaching. This is not in any way a criticism of football coaching – they undoubtedly devote some percentage of their time to working at an individual level as well, but our major focus is totally on one-to-one.

One-to-one coaching

So, one-to-one coaching is judged to be more appropriate to the main criteria we'll be considering in the following chapters.

How does a sports coach work? S/he watches the athlete in action, analysing the actions and identifying the shortfalls. S/he then discusses these identified actions individually with the athlete, pinpointing the shortfall and focusing the athlete's attention on this. Practical experimentation follows.

Coaching outcomes

They both then review possible fine adjustments to achieve improved performance. The athlete practises these particular actions, focusing on including the refinements and striving to improve performance through this fine-tuning. The coach observes the improved actions closely, making further suggestions to help concentrate the learner's focus and efforts even further. Remember, the key to this technique is that coaching involves a learner who already has some degree of competency in the particular skill or knowledge area.

Coaching – Strengths

Coaching:

- empowers the individual to become involved in his/her development;
- requires initial involvement and skill level on the part of the learner;
- encourages active involvement – practical more than theoretical;
- focuses on very specific areas of the learning requirements; and
- allows very clear review of progress from both/all parties involved.

Mentoring

Mentoring is traditionally described as the imparting of wisdom and knowledge by an experienced, influential figure to an inexperienced (and usually younger) individual – or group of individuals. Plato, Aristotle and Confucius were all mentors, with students sitting at their feet absorbing the words of wisdom and discussing matters arising.

Mentoring at University and in Senior Management Development

This one-to-one tutorial activity still happens in a handful of the more established Universities. Mentoring also happens where a young manager is "fast tracked" for promotion by being taken under the wing of a senior manager. One possible outcome may be that the younger high-flyer is going to develop in a very similar mould to the senior manager acting as mentor. There is of course a potential problem here, as there might be imperfections in the senior manager, which we may not necessarily want to be transferred to the next generation model!

What's the difference between mentoring and coaching?

The key difference between mentoring and coaching is that, in mentoring, the two parties will discuss many subject areas about which the learner (or "mentee") knows little, if anything, at the outset. This makes mentoring traditionally more involved in the transfer of knowledge, skills and detail from one who knows to one who initially does not – think of an only partially full, new pitcher being gradually filled from another, larger one, which of course magically remains full!

Mentoring – Strengths

Mentoring:

- encourages discussion and flexible application in the workplace;
- builds rapport between learner (mentee) and more experienced figure;
- can be used to reinforce preferred methods and techniques;
- motivates individual learner to adapt learned skills and knowledge; and
- provides a ready reference point when the learner applies new learning.

Applying the "buddy" system

A special form of mentoring – in a looser definition – is the "buddy" system. With this, a new operative is paired up with a more experienced one, to allow the gradual and appropriate transfer of knowledge and information. As well as being applied within particular businesses, these alliances can also be formed between pairs from different work environments. So, we might have a business manager teaming up with a college or school student – or we could have two individuals as buddies, one in the private and the other in the public sector.

Through fairly informal discussions, the transfer of information and skills can take place – and ways of implementation can be discussed. Yet another form of this buddying, often linked with informal counselling, appears where a young individual is teamed up with an experienced mentor figure to help the young person through the crisis of achieving maturity. This is then crossing over into life coaching territory, which by our definitions will sometimes include elements of mentoring.

Combining the best of all worlds

You've probably spotted that there's not always a firm dividing line between coaching and mentoring. Indeed, some activities might also include elements of tutoring and even bits of formal teaching/training, all mixed together to get the message across most effectively. The name "workplace champion" has been selected as a label that incorporates all these different functions. In all honesty, it's more important that you appreciate the "bigger picture" involvement of as many people as possible and understand the importance of applying as full a range of learning skills as is appropriate to the considered learning needs. The label or name we choose to give to it is really of secondary importance.

The key skills needed to be a workplace champion

Having considered the particular strengths of coaching and mentoring techniques, which you may already have experienced, we now need to focus on the added benefits and skills involved in workplace championing.

The effective champion will have:

- knowledge and experience about specific area(s) of expertise;
- a positive attitude towards helping other people;
- confidence in the support from senior management and the company generally;
- awareness of objectives and how they apply in structured learning;
- competency in getting the message across clearly and precisely;
- experience of reinforcing learning practically, in easily managed sections;
- ability to explain matters in different ways, to overcome "blockages"; and
- skill at keeping records of activities, to ensure continuity and progress.

These are the skills that our champions need to develop and become competent in achieving. Some may already exist in particular initiate champions, to some extent. If so, this is a distinct bonus. Other skills may evolve more slowly. As we're hoping to spread our net wide to involve as many as possible in the process, we must equally be flexible and patient. Workplace championing can and should involve everyone.

Blended learning for best effect

"Blended learning" is the term now widely used to describe the combination of different techniques to meet analysed needs. Add to this the integration of different participants and we get a holistic, "big picture" view of people working supportively

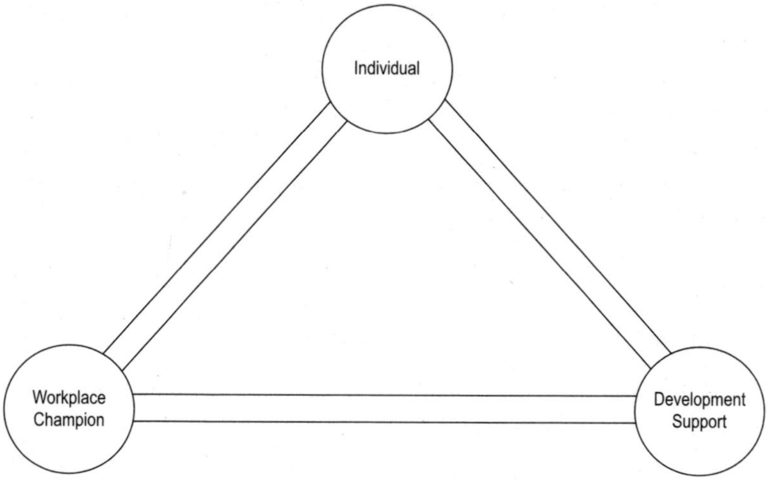

See www. the-integrated-triangle.com

and developmentally with each other. This is the basis of the integrated triangle model, combining the roles of champion, individual learner and development support. Effective workplace championing is key to the success of the model.

Growing our champions

The crucial element when developing the model is to get as many workplace champions as possible applying these listed skills towards helping colleagues develop.

The key message is that a fairly informal championing process offers massive scope for learning to happen rapidly, specifically and cost-effectively, given a positive atmosphere. Some particular training and development will be required to get each workplace champion up to speed, certainly, but this can be kept at a realistic, focused level.

Blending the techniques to make a Workplace Champion

To finally cement the use of the term "Championing" within our blended approach, compare its use with the way we tend to use the term "teaching". Some may still consider good teaching to be the art of the pedagogue, pontificating knowledge to the massed ranks of pupils. Others would see the teacher more as a facilitator encouraging learning to occur in an open, discovery-based environment. We have the gowned Latin master on the one hand, the infant teacher supervising sand and water play on the other.

Embrace the range of learning activities

Our use of the term "Workplace Championing" is a direct parallel, applied in the world of one-to-one, workplace learning and development. It shares some of the important criteria inherent in teaching, such as:

- a structure of learning objectives
- clear and flexible delivery
- practical reinforcement – **performing the activity to apply learned skills**

It is the way forward in an atmosphere where individuals increasingly demand assistance *when* they need it, to maintain progress and achievement of outcomes. Many are no longer content to wait for the next convenient formal training course, which may not be scheduled for several months and need not necessarily totally match their individual needs. Workplace championing is all about this empowerment – being involved in identifying specific needs and providing the learning experience that satisfies those specific needs. That is why we refer to them as "empowered learners", to underline the importance of this involvement.

Focus on workplace championing

So, to review the position so far, what's our workplace champion profile likely to be? S/he's an individual who possesses a level of knowledge and/or skill in a particular area, which s/he can pass on (in a structured though fairly informal way) to another individual who currently possesses less or little knowledge/skill in that particular development area.

Notice – this can centre on very specific competency areas. I might be good at planning and writing reports, for example, with a reasonable command of the English language. So, I might become known as one of the workplace champions you could call upon if you wanted to improve your report writing skills. I, on the other hand, might be completely clueless about Microsoft Excel. If I need to possess at least a basic understanding of how to use this spreadsheet program, in order to produce tables for one of my reports, I would then need to become the individual learner for this information. I would seek out someone within the organisation who was identified as an "Excel Champion", to help me assimilate what I needed to know about the package, become more competent in its application – and most importantly, help me over any on-going hurdles I may meet.

Structured co-operation

It's more than probable that this kind of interaction is already happening in your organisation, in an informal and perhaps limited way. Have you ever been helped by a colleague, for example, when you couldn't remember how to execute a particular computer function? Our goal is to firm up this informal structure and make it more universally acceptable as a learning method. "Firming up", notice – not bogging down in bureaucracy and procedures. A key outcome is to design these championing programmes to be logically structured (and focused at particular learner levels) and then to roll them out progressively within your organisation. Simple? – no … possible? – absolutely!

Dealing with seniority

Earlier, we described the traditional mentor as often being the revered father figure, giving us the idea that the mentor was usually older and more senior than the learner. In our broader champion model it's perfectly feasible for a senior manager to receive input from the office junior, if the new graduate has some specialist knowledge to pass on.

It's quite possible, for example, to have graduate trainees within an organisation who are many times more computer literate than some of the senior management.

Computer literacy perhaps remains something of a generation thing! This informal transfer of tips and techniques happens a lot in the world of ICT, with someone spontaneously helping a colleague by showing them how to carry out some particular operation. It also happens in the world of finance, among others, where interpretation of rules and legislation is passed from the experienced to the less experienced. Applying this information transfer, work can progress and skills and knowledge expand rapidly and responsively. Here we have continuing professional development (CPD) happening spontaneously and co-operatively.

The key result of extending this way of thinking is that we're progressing towards building a very large resource of individual "mini skills specialists". Our network, with a little assistance and a lot of support (both morally and physically), can really broaden the learning and development process within your business or organisation. If handled openly and consistently, workplace championing within the holistic integrated triangle model will progressively generate this resource.

The Bigger Picture

With our broader workplace champion model, we have an activity which:

- involves a mixture of delivering information and coaching in particular skills;
- can elicit information from anyone who is informed enough to be an asset;
- can potentially involve virtually everyone within an organisation;
- requires limited but specific learning transfer skills to ensure effectiveness;
- allows rapid response to meet the identified individual learning shortfalls; and
- potentially covers a high percentage of the learning needs of the organisation.

Is it the answer to every learning need? As we've established-certainly not.

Situations will remain where relatively large groups of people need to be trained at the same time – or the message needs to be totally consistent. An example of this might be training in a system update, or where a large number of new employees have started, who all require the company induction programme.

In these types of cases, a more formal course or presentation would undoubtedly be the answer – although each new employee could also be assigned a champion or "buddy", as a reinforcing follow-on to the formalised input. However, in a situation where there were only one or two new inductees at any given time, workplace championing could be more applicable, allowing a timely message to be presented for each learner. This would be supported by the company providing the resources necessary for that message to come over clearly and consistently.

The purpose in considering blended learning is the realisation that we must mix and match to suit the learner rather than the learning provider. Different learners have different needs and may prefer different techniques. Moreover, some subjects require particular inputs to reinforce the skills. Strictly using only e-learning or text-based methods would not be effective for teaching interpersonal skills, for example.

We've been thinking about workplace championing in general terms so far – now it's time to get more specific. Think of the organisation or business you currently work within – or one that you are aware of. It's time to focus on the way forward.

Focus Time 1.1

Think of the number of people working in your organisation – and their skills. Think of the number of people who still need to learn some of these specific skills – and whose performance is being restricted by reduced competency.

Combine the two together and think of the potential of individuals helping each other.

Think of the positive atmosphere that would make this synergy happen – and what may be necessary within your organisation to be able to "flick on this synergy switch".

Think of some of the support resources which may help to make the whole thing possible. How could you gain access to these resources?

Think what would be necessary to get your workplace champions up to speed.

Think about how you could get involved in the workplace champion process.

Think of the key skills and learning environment, which would be required, in order to pass the information on in this informal, one-to-one way.

That's what we'll be focusing on next.

2 Setting up the Environment

One-minute overview

This chapter ensures that the foundations for the workplace championing model are well and truly in place.
We consider:
- the change in mindset involved;
- the importance of long-term senior management support;
- the applications of a holistic way of thinking;
- the revised role of Training as Development Support; and
- how best to encourage the organisation, development and resource provision for the team of workplace champions.

Applying workplace championing in this way is a bold move. For this reason, planning and preparation are essential.

Changing the mindset

The greatest change in mindset is the belief that virtually everyone can get involved in the development activities, at least to some extent.

Responses to this include:

- "It's not our job – that's what the Training Department's for."
- "I'm no good at explaining things to others."
- "I don't have time to tell other people how to do their jobs."
- "I'm not in a position in this organisation where others will listen to me."
- "What's in it for me?"

These kinds of doubts and responses are to be expected whenever any key change to the status quo is suggested.

Focus Time 2.1

How often have you spent some time – maybe only five or ten minutes – explaining something to somebody else, to allow them to go away and perform that activity, which they could not do prior to your input?

When passing this information on, and it was a subject about which you felt well informed, how easy did you find it to get the message across? When there was a problem with the learner understanding something you were describing, could you explain things in different ways?

Having been on a particular training course, how often have you hit a snag in trying to apply some of the ideas back in the workplace – and how often was that snag sorted out by someone more experienced giving you a few tips and suggestions?

Can you think of occasions when your progress at work has been slowed down, either because you don't know how to do something – or because you're waiting for someone else to complete something that your progress depends upon? These are the kinds of blockages that can be "unstuck" by an injection of championing to resolve the delay.

Ten minutes spent by a champion who knows the business will get you moving again – as opposed to you potentially spending hours trying to solve issues and problems on your own.

Foundations

There are several basic foundation structures that must be in place to allow the successful construction of the entire Workplace Championing model.

The most important of these foundation elements is consistent company support, represented by senior management.

The lack of consistent management support: the time management example

Picture the scene – an in-company time-management training programme designed specially for a major oil company, in response to a key management development initiative. On one of the courses for middle management, a senior manager knocks on the door to call a delegate out of the course to do something that he (the senior manager) had forgotten about. That single action effectively overshadowed all further discussions on prioritisation, planning and delegation at a stroke. The tutor should have told the senior manager to go away – and then used the interruption as a teaching point – but was conscious that the manager would undoubtedly receive the ultimate corporate support if the matter came to a head. This example shows there was a lack of consistency between what the senior management in the organisation expected and what they actually did in practice.

Establishing firm guidelines to workplace championing

It is essential to establish firm guidelines to workplace championing before progressing with any planned sea-change development. Otherwise, the long-term initiative is likely to fail, with a resultant waste of time, money, patience, trust and resources. And once it has been seen to fail, the likelihood of getting a second chance to launch is limited. The programme must be seen to succeed with the initial initiative.

Establishing and supporting workplace champion learning

Senior management need to both see and support the long-term vision relating to the planned application of workplace championing in the organisation.

Benefits of Workplace Championing

Workplace championing means:

- the transfer of information happens time-economically;
- the detailed training is specific to the direct business needs;
- the operational problem is solved immediately, allowing progress;
- the potential for follow-up consolidation of the learning is established;
- positive team interactions are encouraged;

- a possible vehicle for fault-finding and fine-tuning departmental processes is being developed; and
- a cost-effective solution to staff development is in operation.

The "7 Cs" of integrated management

There's a lot spoken about developing leadership skills in managers – with some effort being put into attempting to reproduce the unique skills distilled from successful entrepreneurs. This is immediately threatening to create a second-hand, second-rate training facsimile and is misunderstanding what the key criteria of management leadership are all about. Real entrepreneurs are unique individuals, who succeed to some large extent because they are uniquely different. They can't be packaged – indeed some apparently successful entrepreneurs have a fairly chequered success-rate, longer-term. Using the management-speak of the moment, we're looking more for a "big picture" than a "blue skies" thinker.

The "big picture" thinking manager

Put simply, the "big picture thinking" manager should be capable of applying and reinforcing our integrated, co-operative workplace model if s/he is:

- ***competent***
- ***consistent***
- ***conversant***
- ***credible***
- ***creative***
- ***communicative***
- ***co-operative***

These are considered to be the key criteria for setting up and maintaining an integrated, co-operative approach to management – which is all-important for maintaining the consistency of the championing progress. Senior managers require continuing professional development just the same as everyone else. There will of course be a stronger demand for the detail to be very specific to the individual's needs – and that any sessions for the transfer of information are carried out one-to-one at an appropriate time. These are all features of workplace championing – making the technique equally appropriate for senior staff, as long as the selected champions are credible. Direct, successful involvement in the process is bound to encourage long-term support.

Building a synergy

If wide-scale workplace championing can become company policy; if the concept of people helping each other informally within the workplace is seen as positive progress; if long-term involvement in the overall process is encouraged; if senior managers not only support the initiative but become directly involved themselves as champions: then there is the potential for a synergy to build and develop within the organisation.

It's a large-scale change ... some may even call it a paradigm ... so it won't happen overnight. Slowly and steadily, however, it will move forward. The secret is to initially focus on manageable pilot schemes, which can be progressively nursed towards successful conclusions. These in turn become examples on which larger schemes are modelled ... and so the structure builds.

This represents the holistic approach, bringing that all-important "value added" to both the performance and ethos of the working environment.

The holistic approach to workplace development

Holistic is defined as "the formation of wholes in nature which are more than the sum of the parts by ordered grouping". In real terms, this means that, when you combine a range of individual actions positively and co-operatively, the resulting outcome gives an overall impact which is more effective than the sum of these individual actions.

Holistic team building

Applying a holistic approach to combining the key skills of individual team members, you achieve a team outcome which goes beyond what you might expect from the outputs of the same bunch of people, acting as individuals. (This might be for activities such as planning and producing a presentation, report or project, for example.) An effective, positively managed workplace-championing programme will generate this co-operative atmosphere – which results in additional valuable knock-on effects. That's added value!

Action Time 2.1

We've already established that support from senior management is a key foundation.

From your current understanding of setting up such a learning environment, think of at least three other foundation elements which you would consider to be important, to permit championing to work effectively.

Make a note of these separately. Complete this before you read further.

Additional components

Possible answers to the above action time include:

- some training in communicating the message clearly;
- help and support in planning the learning/championing detail;
- the availability of resources to help you explain things;
- a data bank/reference source to find details of other champions etc; and
- an overall organisation to help arrange and record the activities and outcomes.

You may have given other answers – the key picture which is emerging is one where there is a need for support and encouragement, as well as resources being readily available. This will both help our workplace championing happen ... and ensure that it is consistently allowed to develop positively and progressively. This consistency is key!

Action Time 2.2

Imagine that you are already a workplace champion.

From your awareness so far, what support would you think was most important?

Make a note of your ideas elsewhere.

In general terms, senior management support has already been identified. What specifically would you be looking for from these senior managers?

Make a note of your key ideas before reading further.

Possible answers include:

It's important that:

- time is allowed for development activities to take place;
- senior managers suggest that specific championing events occur *and* get involved as champions themselves;
- support is given to identify or create resources;
- the need for follow-up consolidation is supported consistently;
- resources are made available and supplied for the champion to use;
- help is available for champions to develop their own resources;
- there is a generally supportive atmosphere from other departments;
- the transfer of required skills operates throughout the organisation; and
- the organisation is seen as supporting those involved as key players.

It is relevant to underline at this point that virtually every job description for a post at middle or senior management level includes some permutation of the phrase "has responsibility for the training and development of reporting staff". This involvement should now be in the job description of EVERY employee in the whole organisation.

Finding time for workplace championing to happen, both on and off-site, is undoubtedly a managerial responsibility. Positively supporting the short injections of time necessary for workplace championing activities to take place is, as we've already stressed, a key example of the active support which is required from management.

The training department as the development support function

Inevitably there is a need to change the way people in the organisation think.

We are, for example, asking the Training Department to be more of a support agency, becoming a major part of the "Development Support Function" (DSF) identified in the Integrated Triangle model. This supporting role will reinforce the training-based activities of the champions, whom the DSF might not immediately relate to as being "professional trainers".

Historically some people have tended to talk in a rather disparaging way about on-the-job-training, often described as "sitting with Nellie". Nellie was seen as being the long-time employee who knew how to do things and could train a new starter. This is fine in principle. However, many of these "Nellies" managed to maintain quality standards in their own work, while applying short cuts and other techniques to manipulate the system. Training Departments rightly consider it important that, from the outset, new starters learn the officially prescribed way to carry out processes. Lack of the necessary experience meant that most new starts couldn't cope with the short cuts which some "Nellies" (perhaps unconsciously) included in their training – so standards were inclined to suffer.

Learning from this past experience of on-the-job training, we can identify this as one of the key areas considered important in the initial training of champions. Development programmes must ensure that our champions are clear of the competencies, processes and objective standards that they will be transferring to others. Where company processes and procedures are in place, these must be reinforced. This will then reflect on the techniques and programmes applied – and the methods used to assess progress.

Building a widespread resource base

If the Training Department can accept that a workplace championing system will allow them to build up a wide and varied support team – they will be able to tap into a potentially vast resource. Additional champions will come on board as the system establishes itself, providing scope for offering quick learning injections covering an ever-widening range of skills. The champions will evidently require specific training in planning and delivery, to meet any individual shortfalls identified. Direct involvement in this specific training should allow the Training Department to feel they are maintaining some degree of control over the quality of service. Championing activities such as coaching and mentoring will, of course, be integrated with other, more formalised learning techniques to provide as wide a toolkit as possible.

The need for overall organisation

A workplace-championing programme does require overall organisation, as well as the monitoring and recording of detail of activities; it will also require the Training Department to become more supportive, as a resource provider. This involves the DSF in taking on a more proactive supporting role. Can one support proactively? Most certainly, if there is awareness of the potential needs of both champions and individual learners.

How do you do this? By communicating with them.

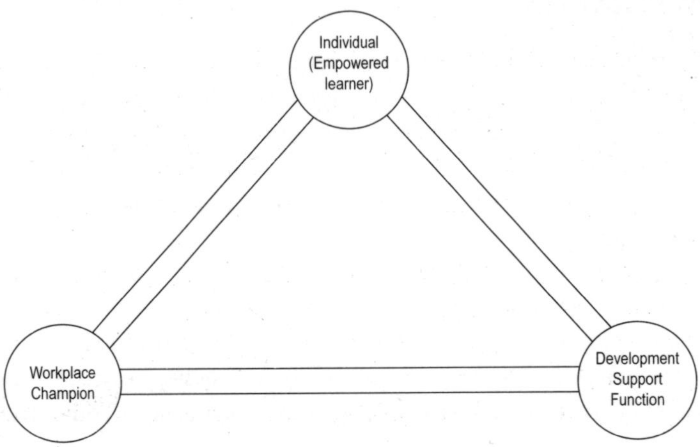

The relationships – and inter-relationships – should be becoming clearer.

Communication by the Integrated Triangle approach

We've now introduced all three corners of the integrated triangle to our discussions regarding developing the workplace-championing model.

The relationships – and inter-relationships – should be becoming clearer.

Growing a team of champions

Developing a team of champions takes time. As well as the focused training involved, there is:

- the construction of the skills base and the network of individuals to service it;
- the ongoing identification and supply of resources;
- the shadow (buddying) support of the first activities; and
- the "rapid response" assistance necessary to overcome early blockages.

Concentrating on achieving these will ensure that any teething troubles are resolved.

Maintaining credibility

Throughout this process, the championing programme must maintain its credibility. As we've already emphasised, this comes through ensuring that the first events are successful. Only one thing travels faster than good news – and that's bad news! It is essential that the word is spread positively, encouraging more people to try this new self-supported approach of individual development. As with the early stages of any large-scale development programme, it's crucial that the initial momentum can be maintained.

Progressing consistently will allow the organisation to reach the critical mass point – when general interest and enthusiasm will take over and involvement will expand naturally.

Ensuring the expansion

We can:

- Help this to some degree by selecting champions for the initial activities who have had some prior experience of working constructively with others.
- Choose to focus our initial activities in a department (or small group of departments) where we know the senior management is supportive of the idea of one-to-one development.
- Feel more confident that, in these situations, everyone will stick with the programme through any initial glitches.
- Identify our initial empowered learners as those whom we can expect to respond favourably to this form of training and development.

This may seem marginally manipulative but decisions like these will give a stronger guarantee of success in the opening initiatives. It's all part of building those necessary strong foundations – and flagging up successes.

Keeping track

Being realistic, a widespread championing programme will encompass a broad range of levels of enthusiasm. At the top end, there are the individuals active in their own development who can virtually drive themselves. With some initial assistance, they will identify their own areas for development in their work, seek out (directly or through data banks) suitable champions to assist with their particular shortfalls – and prioritise and arrange for the learning and reinforcement to take place. This is the ideal and it is empowering.

The middle range of people – probably the majority – will need a greater degree of encouragement to keep moving forward. As usual, this can come through regular reviews and appraisals. The model is probably more concerned about informally encouraging these individuals to view their performance more critically and objectively, within a blame-free atmosphere.

Freedom from blame

This freedom from blame is important. Few people would be prepared to identify and discuss with their boss what they perceive as their own weaknesses, if they felt in any way that he/she would use knowledge of these facts against them. We all have weaknesses but we may develop them into strengths using this model of personal development.

Time management – Another example

Iain's time management problems, for example, may be caused not by his personal inefficiency but by his boss regularly landing last-minute requests on his desk. Iain may have followed best practice and have a pre-planned schedule for his day. Even though this should have included flexible sectors for responding to emergency activities, he is likely to experience problems in incorporating these additional requests regularly. When they arrive towards the close of the working day, they become even more unacceptable – and are an indication of the boss's rather than Iain's inefficiency at time management. The two of them need to discuss the issue – again within a blame-free atmosphere. In this situation, the development need can become one of communication rather than time management.

Establishing specific needs

So, when specific development needs occur, it is essential to be able to discuss them openly with colleagues, in order to pinpoint priorities and interactions. This suggests that one person's development needs may indicate related development needs in others – for instance there's little point in Iain considering the skills involved in prioritisation if his boss is going to continue to dash in at the last minute, demanding rush jobs, pulling rank and in effect overturning any learned procedures regarding standard prioritisation that Iain might have been applying.

Discussing these situations in a 360° way, with Iain potentially giving as much input as his boss, requires a certain degree of objectivity. However, if the total problem can't be exposed, objectively discussed and hopefully resolved through such "in the round" reviews, the existing problem will continue to bump along from one crisis to the next. This is the atmosphere that must be encouraged in the preparatory stages of setting up a championing model. It's only if such needs analysis and problem solving can operate freely and consistently that we can build and maintain an overall atmosphere of credibility. However, you need to be aware that many people do find criticism harder to receive than give, so this is a difficult learning curve for many and you may find some of your team will require additional support here.

Plan prior to action

In order for any development plans to be successful, it's crucial that the foundations and operating parameters are in place before trying to elicit change through any form of training. Trying to build a new operational model such as workplace championing without the required support in place will not work. It will de-motivate everyone concerned – be a waste of time and money and will kill a wonderful opportunity for staff development. Devote the necessary time to getting the championing infrastructure right initially and you will have a much stronger likelihood of success. Initial positive attitudes to developing a new training technique are much more important than immediately focusing on training the skills.

Providing the support

So, this level of monitoring, support and direction must be provided by someone. The overall championing of the new strategy must come from the top – and must be allowed time to flourish. This is no place for short-term, flavour-of-the-month thinking – we're looking for that consistent, credible support from managers who are seen to be competent by their immediate workforce. As the content and priorities become more specific to each section or department, the learning responses will be perceived as being more valid. They are also more likely to be seen as specific to individual and workplace needs – if delivered from within the department itself.

The workplace-championing programme will also work more successfully if seen by all as being the direct responsibility of a relatively senior manager or supervisor. In some companies, the heads of department like to monitor progress personally, while in others, the supervisor or team leader is given the role. It's not complex – if you have a list of the operational and knowledge skills and competencies (as provided within Vocational Qualification criteria, for example), you have a reference list to compare the individual's strengths and shortfalls against. Remember that, by applying Continuing Professional Development in this age of specialisation, we're increasingly concerned with keeping the specialist's key skills sharp and up-to-date, rather than necessarily trying to constantly broaden his skills base.

Having on-going monitoring and support represented at senior level in the organisation maintains the momentum and purpose for this overall professional development process.

Record keeping

Of course, some training and development involvement and responses are dictated by legislation – or to meet across-the-board company criteria – so the need for centralised record keeping for these issues remains very important. Health and Safety issues, initial induction and awareness of company policies are all examples of this, where we must record that individuals have met the objectives of the particular programmes. Some of these might possibly be disseminated using a wide range of workplace champions – however, maintaining records of completion is a standard HR/training requirement and would therefore continue to be administered by this department ultimately. Some operational departments may also wish to hold duplicate records.

The record keeping which is more relevant to our considerations at this point is that relating to the champions rather than the individual learners. Initially, some large degree of effort is put into identifying champions to support particular skills and areas of knowledge. Many of these individuals may be known within their own department – but not throughout the organisation, so a data bank approach makes sure that the range of support is captured for rapid future reference across the board.

Building the data system

When building a system, it may be more realistic to concentrate initially on amassing departmental lists of champions, to be used initially within each "parent" department. The championing time involvement is easier to justify and also accept, if seen to be improving the efficiency and output of the department in which both the learner and the champion are involved. It's certainly more likely to receive support from the senior managers within that department if they can see these direct benefits. This is another example of starting small and specific in order to ensure a greater likelihood of initial success.

In time, specialist transfer of particular skills and knowledge areas may be shared across departmental boundaries ... but it's best to take it one step at a time!

From foundations to building blocks

So far, we've been concentrating on getting the foundations of our workplace championing model as firm and secure as possible. This, after all, is practising what we have been preaching. Two of the key criteria we have been repeatedly reinforcing are:

- confident competency and
- consistency

We're looking for this in our champions – and through the support all receive throughout the organisation. Openness and holistic attitudes will help to cement these criteria, and enable us to build our workplace champion framework.

3 Focus on Growing

One-minute overview

This chapter looks closely at what it takes to become a workplace champion, including the Ten Prime Skills and the identification processes involved. It looks at the degree of structure required and the importance of applying a range of techniques and resources through blended learning. It considers a range of reasons which underline the benefits of applied workplace championing.

Now that we've established our key foundation requirements, we can concentrate on the "growing" part of our title. Here we will look at the "bigger picture" in a holistic way – establishing how we can develop a range of skills which "produce a result that is greater than the sum of its parts". This is the general definition of holistic – in the case of workplace championing, this means that the overall effect and effectiveness of the championing process on both learners and their department is greater than we might expect from a range of individual learning sessions. This chapter will concentrate on the skills and criteria involved in developing (or "growing") workplace champions, in order that they can contribute to this holistic end result.

Key components for becoming a workplace champion

Remember our priorities – the overall purpose is to develop a network of champions as people who can impart identified blocks of information, gradually helping other individuals to develop their competency levels. The pay-back is that any particular champion can in turn expect help at different times from others acting as champions, to improve some of his/her learning shortfalls. So, on some occasions, you can be a champion helping others; at other times, you will be the learner, receiving information from someone else acting as champion. This is the holistic network effect.

The intention is to get as many people as possible involved in being champions – some perhaps only imparting some very specific skill, while others may choose to become involved in a broader range of learning activities. Champions will succeed through applying a combination of mentoring, coaching and related workplace learning skills, often delivered at a fairly informal level. Later chapters in this book will consider many of these skills, to allow the reader to learn and apply the techniques. It's likely that some extra assistance will be required by many new champions, to allow them to convert some of the ideas into practice. In effect, you may need help from an existing champion, competent in championing skills, in order to make you confident enough to become involved as a champion yourself!

Key Championing Components

In terms of delivery skills, champions will primarily be working one-to-one with single learners. Therefore, they:

- will be discussing or facilitating detail rather than lecturing or presenting;
- will need to select knowledge and language levels to suit each learner;

- will include periodic practical exercises to reinforce learning interactively;
- will also apply this consolidation during subsequent normal work experience;
- are concerned primarily with the content and application of the learning;
- will check regularly by questioning, that the learner is understanding the detail; and
- will follow a logical sequence of learning steps towards a defined end objective.

Action Time 3.1

Referring to these key championing components, think of as many competencies (or capabilities) as you can, which you would consider to be important for someone carrying out the role of workplace champion. Note them separately.

Detailed skills analysis for the champion

While some of these in your list will be skills that can be – or have been – learned, others are likely to be innate to some people. Part of the initial process of developing a champion will involve establishing his/her individual strengths and shortfalls.

This might require detailed discussions, to ensure that the new champion can relate knowledge of their own character to the particular activities involved in acting as a workplace champion for other people. Some skilled operators, for example, find it very hard to appreciate the difficulty that novices have in completing the activities which they do routinely – and often without much thought. They can therefore have a problem in "getting down to the level" of the empowered learner's understanding.

Example 1: Driver training

This learning level issue can be a key communication breakdown. You may, for example, be a car driver of many years who has offered to sit with a learner driver while he's training to drive. Simple. You drive virtually every day … and can change gear as easily as you can change your clothes.

However, when the learner consistently judders to a stalled halt on trying to move away from the kerb, you may well have found that it's quite difficult to pinpoint exactly what the learner driver's doing wrong.

It is essential to be able to analyse the learning process and then describe the steps and sequence of achieving a smooth transfer up through the gears from a standing start. And even when you've analysed the steps, tips and techniques, you may find it difficult to explain this in clear, bite-sized chunks of information – and identify and coach the elements which are causing the problem. For the car-driving example, this is likely to be the control in letting out the clutch and the point at which the actions of the clutch and accelerator interact.

If you can't understand why someone is doing something wrong, first picture what they are trying to achieve as the end result of a process, and then visualise that process as a series of steps or gradual movements. Talk through each of the stages, how they connect to each other as a sequence, and how best to achieve each one – including any special techniques you know of.

Competency requirement

So, the champion has to be able to –

- analyse the activity to establish the sequence of steps and stages;
- clearly define these steps and stages;

- express the detail in manageable segments (the "bite-sized chunks");
- present the information at an understandable level;
- pinpoint the stage in the sequence where the learner has a problem; and
- coach for improvement.

Example 2 - Computer operation

Consider this analysis when applied to activities such as computer keyboard instruction. The experienced operator will often "demonstrate" the various keystroke commands very rapidly and then assume that the learner will have picked up the sequence. As a new champion involved in training, the experienced operator may find real difficulty in remembering the steps as discrete stages in the process, to be demonstrated separately. S/he may need some encouragement to sit down with pen and paper to analyse and list them. S/he may also need reminding that it's not enough to just demonstrate – there must be stages where the individual learner is actually practising the new skill directly.

The Workplace Champion – The Ten Key Competencies

So, to identify and develop a potential workplace champion, what key competencies would we agree are important? Some of these will be innate to some degree – others will certainly require development.

S/he must be -

1. patient, coupled with a calm disposition;
2. able to plan detail logically;
3. capable of explaining complex detail in an unambiguous way;
4. even-tempered, to maintain levels of learner encouragement;
5. skilled and experienced in his/her selected specialist areas;
6. able to specify objectives clearly and relate to their application;
7. informed about a range of applicable learning techniques, perhaps from study or previous experience as learner or informal tutor;
8. clear about the importance of workplace reinforcement of the learning;
9. capable of setting up effective practical reinforcement exercises – and have the facilities (such as a computer, perhaps with internet connection) available to do this; and
10. aware of the relationships between what is being taught and areas of knowledge, skills, software etc. to which it connects – such as applying general inter-personal skills to the specific needs in contact centre or particular service industry.

How many of these do you identify with? Are there any additional ones which you would consider to be important?

Developing champions

Remember, we're trying to build as wide a selection of active workplace champions as possible. So, we're not going to reject people who don't totally meet the criteria. Potential champions who have particular technical skills or knowledge should be developed or "grown" to be able to impart this information to others. Some will require more development than others. Some may be able to become operational merely by studying and applying the content of this book. Others may require specific coaching from a facilitator informed about the principles of the integrated triangle model.

Some of the competencies listed above – (probably the first five) – are the types of innate skills which we would seek out when initially identifying our champions. Others are skills which are more likely to require some additional training or coaching. As the champion grows progressively, it is likely that s/he will require some additional input for the majority of the areas listed.

In attempting to involve as many people as possible as workplace champions, we must be prepared to accept these innate skills at varying levels of competence. There may, for example, be an acknowledged subject specialist who might be a little impatient with others – or find it difficult to understand why a learner has difficulties in learning and applying his specialist subject. Although he is evidently not "the ideal teacher", with some assistance in achieving most of the key championing competencies listed previously, he could become a very valuable member of the champion team (perhaps for working with more senior or advanced learners).

Competency Shortfalls

Discussing specific strengths and shortfalls with each champion will lead to the identification of shortfall areas which s/he would have to develop further, in order to become a more effective champion. It may be impracticable to expect to be able to improve all shortfall areas. For example, a particular champion may be able to describe policies and procedures clearly – but be very poor at producing and using visuals to illustrate what s/he means. In terms of on-going development, we could consider it more important that this particular champion keeps up-to-date with changes and amendments to the policies and procedures – while accepting that her/his visuals may be at a rather amateur level. Increasingly, CPD (continuing professional development) in business will be focusing on improving and updating currently required skills rather than constantly expanding into new skills. Depth is deemed more important than breadth.

Highlighting competency shortfalls in our champions

So, if we're looking for widespread championing involvement, we'll have to accept that some shortfalls in the personality of the champion can probably not be greatly improved. Take *patience*, for example. This is certainly a virtue that we'd like to have present. However, think back to your school days. Can you recall any teachers who you would rate as being effective – who really managed to bring their subject alive? Perhaps your job specialisation in adulthood may even be the direct result of the inspiration which this teacher imparted to you? However, was s/he a consistent paragon of patience? Perhaps not. But you were still motivated and inspired.

Referring to the list again, some competencies will be more important than others.

Focus Time 3.1

Let's consider each of the listed competency areas in turn. For the purpose of the exercise, put yourself in the position of helping in the identification and development of new champions ... bearing in mind that you'll probably be one of them!

1. Being patient with learners

This is what we're looking for in anyone involved in teaching and training others as a champion, applying the vast range of techniques (including coaching and mentoring). However patient someone is, s/he will have off-days – or will be distracted by other pressures or concerns. This can be a problem for the full-time teacher or trainer – it may be more of a problem for a champion with additional operational responsibilities within the organisation. However, our champion has more opportunity than the full-time teacher to be able to select the best time for the learning exchange to take place ... or even to postpone the learning session if the time is evidently not right.

Choosing the best time for learning

An informal approach to training others allows for flexibility. As a workplace champion, if you're preoccupied with a work problem you should seek to get this resolved before working with your learner. This will allow you to focus on and give importance to the transfer of skills and knowledge, rather than rushing things impatiently in order to get finished and back to "your real job". Speedy, thoughtless delivery is not something we wish to develop – so choose your times and put your heart into it!

One of the other benefits of workplace championing under this "patience" heading is that we can normally spread the learning and reinforcement over a longer period of time than is possible with classroom teaching. This allows the new information to be consolidated within the workplace experiences as they occur, building the champion's confidence as s/he sees the new learning being applied effectively. It also allows for any additional remedial recaps, to re-explain some of the detail which may not have been fully understood by the learner.

2. Thinking logically as a champion

Learning should progress in steps and stages – like building bricks one on top of the other. People who are pragmatists or theorists naturally think in these logical sequences. They can therefore see these separate "bricks" and how they build progressively together. As a workplace champion, think in developmental stages – the baby crawls, before s/he walks, before s/he runs. Visualise these developmental stages for your learner as well. S/he should, for example, learn the basic detail first, before seeing an operation being demonstrated slowly, before s/he ultimately tries it her/himself.

Learning sequences

There is usually a natural sequence to doing things – but this doesn't necessarily mean you always follow the sequence from A to Z. Logical sequences instil a little order into life – but applied lateral creativity is valuable as well. As champion, you can, for example, allow your activist learner to experiment to discover the best way for him/her to achieve something. You should however be fairly clear in your own mind how the learning event might progress – and be very clear as to what the expected outcome should be. So, the creativity is channelled logically, towards an identified outcome. This involves a combination of left and right brain thinking ... applying both hemispheres appropriately. Creativity, sequence and focused outcome – all are equally necessary.

Champions should try to picture the development of the learning sequence by following the natural progression of a process. Take a simple domestic example of setting and lighting a multi-fuel stove (which some people find difficulty in achieving).

Start at the base and work upwards.

10. ***Add coal/anthracite/logs periodically.***
9. ***Monitor/control draught until ignited material has stabilised.***
8. ***Open door and add logs/coal – re-close fire door and reduce draught.***
7. ***Allow fire to flare brightly until coal/anthracite has ignited.***
6. ***Open draught vent or ashtray door to create draught.***
5. ***Light paper and close fire door.***
4. ***Place pieces of coal/anthracite on kindling.***
3. ***Crumple paper and add kindling on top.***
2. ***Collect dry kindling and newspaper.***
1. ***Clear ash from grate and ashtray.***

Key tips and techniques for operation

- Ash must be cleared to permit draught.
- Kindling (firewood) must be dry and plentiful.
- Use actual pieces of coal/anthracite, do not smother fire with lots of coal dust.
- Allow plenty of draught until material has ignited totally.
- Add extra logs/coal etc once stabilised, to maintain the "heart" of the fire.

Knowing the important stages of the sequence – and key tips and techniques – will help you monitor the learner's progress and understand why (or even why not) s/he is improving. This will also provide indicators of areas of information or skills which may need additional emphasis or repetition during follow-up remedial and consolidation inputs.

Applying structure in a less formal learning situation

Sometimes, we can apply thinking or ideas from a more formal way of working to the less formal learning situation we are creating through workplace championing. For example, most people will accept the need to have minutes of a formal meeting, to confirm agreed outcomes. Now, think less formally. If you have a conversation in the corridor, emailing your colleague subsequently with your understanding of the agreed action will have a similar effect, following the same principles.

In this example, the learner is likely to be aware of the general logic of formal meeting minutes – so will be more likely to accept the extension of the concept to include informal email confirmation, applying similar logical steps. This is part of thinking in the "bigger picture", where solutions can be established which are modelled on parallel, more formal business and training activities.

Supporting the sequences of practical learning

There are many exercises, case studies, questionnaires and other resources which the champion can use to reinforce the detail of any learning session. The business sections of good bookshops are a good source. Within business itself, assistance in providing these supporting resources can be expected from the various responsibilities making up what we refer to as the "Development Support Function (DSF)". This DSF will include levels of responsible management, technical support, the training department and personnel/HR. When selecting from these various resources, however, you must make sure that they meet and reinforce your identified learning needs clearly.

This is achieved through the champion being clearly aware of the intended outcome (or objective) of the learning session. Through this focus, you'll be able to judge how effective any available resource would be in reinforcing this outcome. Being aware of the expected outcome or objective will put you in a better position to identify the detail which is missing in the content of any resource. You can then either find a more appropriate resource or do something about creating or sourcing supplementary material to bridge the identified information gaps. We will consider learning objectives and the selection of supporting resources in chapters dedicated to these subjects later in this book.

Remember the new perceived role of the Training Department and others as Development Support Function (DSF). They're there to help the workplace champions in both the analysis and delivery of the learning sessions. The clearer you are, as a workplace champion, about outcomes, content and required reinforcement, the more inclined the DSF members should be towards helping you. In order to expect professionalism from them, the champion must also endeavour to be as professional as possible.

3. Explaining information and concepts clearly to the learner

Being competent in this communication skill is certainly one of the key criteria of being a good teacher or champion. Compare the extremes likely in the championing process. On the one hand, we might have someone who is a real expert in the skill – but who can't explain the detail at a level which the individual learner can understand. On the other, we could have someone who is a good communicator, although not experienced in this particular skill, so less capable of imparting the real expertise and techniques involved.

In developing workplace champions, we're concentrating on taking people who are skilled operators or informed experts and helping them work at the learner's level of understanding. To do this, they must present the information in such a way that the learning and reinforcement can be assimilated and applied by the learner in manageable "bite-sized chunks" of detail.

Explaining the message clearly

What are some of the ways of delivering this information clearly?

- Following the logical sequence of learning steps and stages.
- Maintaining consistent rules and detail from one session to the next.
- Using simple language – keeping jargon to a minimum and, where technical language does have to be used, explaining it.
- Getting the information across in manageable "bite-sized chunks".

- Remaining aware of the learner and re-explaining, probably in a different (more considered) way, any areas of confusion.
- Using illustrations, practical models and real examples to demonstrate ideas.
- Getting the learner involved through practical activities and discussion etc.

How do we initially check whether a potential champion is capable of explaining things clearly? Simple – ask him/her to explain something which is new to us and see how much we understand. If we don't understand a particular description, interrupt and ask for a clearer explanation. How do they cope? Can they re-explain in a different, more coherent way? If this is done when encouraging and coaching new workplace champions, it should help them to see learning from the learner's viewpoint – and to respond more actively to particular individual needs and areas of potential confusion.

4. Taking an even-tempered approach in championing

This is associated with *patience* above - but it goes further. Can your potential champion think positively and accept the fact that the empowered learner is really *trying* to learn. If so, s/he will understand that any lapse of understanding is not because s/he is stupid or troublesome – but is more likely to be because the message is not being presented clearly – and/or is not seen as relevant.

Again, the workplace champion is more likely to stay even-tempered if s/he's set aside the time to devote to the coaching/mentoring activity. Through doing this, there should be few if any outside pressures interfering with the championing task in hand. Through maintaining an atmosphere of even-temperedness, the workplace champion will encourage the rapport and confidence which is considered very important in developing each champion/learner relationship.

Selection for the initial pilot programme

Although we can set the conditions to encourage as even-tempered an approach as possible, being even-tempered is to some extent a natural trait. Initial pilot programmes *must* be seen to succeed, to encourage expansion and support for the future workplace championing programme. It is important therefore, when selecting the initial team of workplace champions, to strive to identify individual champions who are inclined towards being naturally patient and even-tempered. This will give a stronger guarantee that our first championing activities will be a success.

Having flexible expectations when identifying champions

Remember, we're trying to get as many people as possible involved in championing. If we're trying to involve (virtually) everyone, we must be aware that some are less even-tempered than others. Some will therefore require greater assistance to enable them to appreciate the variations in understanding, attention span, interest and general competency present between learners – leading towards them being able to respond appropriately.

Think of the teachers you had at school. You undoubtedly had some fairly bad tempered ones – but still learned a lot about their subjects. This may have been encouraged by a slight fear element, which is, after all, another form of motivation! Thus, although having an even temper is a trait to strive for, champions displaying less than perfect patience can still become very effective champions, especially for learners who may benefit from tighter control.

Encouraging championing in your organisation

Given a co-operative atmosphere, most people can potentially act as workplace champions. Some will of course succeed more naturally than others. There will certainly be different "skill injections" necessary to respond to the wide range of possible shortfalls, including the even-temperedness we've been reviewing. These skill inputs will happen over time. Some will be gained through books and other resources. Others will be best achieved through direct learning sessions – either by attending courses or through coaching/mentoring from specialist facilitators, using the same one-to-one championing techniques.

The SERIOUS benefits of a workplace championing approach

By this stage, the huge potential that this integrated development resource can offer to participating organisations should be clear. We're proposing an ever-developing team of champions which is:

skilled – *in their particular specialisms*
effective – *in both time and training outcomes*
reciprocal – *involved in both giving and receiving learning*
informed – *about both their subject and its delivery*
objective – *about learning outcomes and inter-relationships*
unified – *in techniques, message and mission*
spontaneous – *about providing inputs as and when required*

Applying these separate competencies holistically will create an overall effect where knowledge and skills can be shared throughout the organisation, providing enhanced effects. Specific inputs and reinforcement can be delivered more responsively than through traditional training solutions; operational momentum can be maintained.

5. Selecting areas of subject speciality

It can be reasonably assumed that everyone with experience of working in a particular environment possesses some percentage of the necessary specialist subject skills and/or knowledge which make them employable. Some will feel more confident than others in applying these specialist areas – or perhaps admitting publicly to the degree of competence which they possess. There may of course be occasional individuals whose confidence is greater than their competence!

Focus Time 3.2 – Selecting your own specialist areas

Here is an exercise to try. Your answers should be your first, immediate responses, without considering relative reasons behind the questions. So, give your responses first – then we'll consider the outcomes and purpose of the exercise.

This exercise is inviting you to think of your own skills and shortfalls. If it helps, make some notes separately.

Focus on your skills first. These are areas which you really feel you are competent in achieving. It could be a technical skill, such as the ability to produce impressive PowerPoint™ presentations, complete with imported graphics and photographs. It could be an interpersonal skill, such as being good at negotiating WIN-WIN outcomes at meetings. You decide. Think of four or five – then rank them in order.

Now, do the same with your personal shortfalls. Again, think of four or five. These might be areas such as difficulties with time management, or problems with recalling specific detail, in the longer-term. Think of them in relation to achieving your workplace outcomes on a day-to-day basis. Some may be more of a problem than others. Highlight the shortfalls that are holding you back in some way. These are the ones you must address, face-on. You may be able to offload some of the others – that's the value of delegation, as long as your remaining specialist skills continue to make you indispensable!

OK, so what outcome can you apply as a result of your responses?

In the first, Skill section, you're giving first considerations as to the particular skills and/or knowledge which you could transfer to someone who doesn't possess them. These are the initial activities in which you might become involved as a workplace champion.

In the second, Shortfall section, you are selecting specific areas where you, as an individual learner, would be looking for some additional input to improve your competency levels. Some of these will be key areas which you identify as being necessary to meet your objectives (and targets, if these enter the equation as well).

Matching champions and learners

Can you imagine a data bank containing a grid with the names of people who require help in achieving specific skills levels, interfacing with another grid identifying people who are competent in sharing or championing these skills? Match champion with learner within the department – and the learning process can begin almost immediately. With appropriate support and organisation, the scope is vast. Think about this potential for a moment – that's synergy for you ... that's the holistic outcome in action!

6. Having a clear awareness about objectives and their application

This is an important issue.

Think about reaching an objective – or an outcome – or a goal. The more specific you can be about what it is you're trying to achieve, the clearer you will be about what you have to do in order to achieve it. This is the essence of establishing the content of the learning session.

Being clear about your end objective or goal will also help you assess *when* both you and the learner have actually achieved it satisfactorily. We can probably all think about business examples where confusion results from the fact that manager and staff member have different understandings of what the outcome or goal actually involves, having insufficiently or poorly discussed it. The same can be true with learning objectives for trainers and learners. For this reason, it's important that learning objectives are as specific as possible.

Stating objectives and outcomes

Learning objectives are written in terms of actions – what the learner must DO to achieve the specified outcome. Notice that – the learner, NOT the workplace champion or coach/mentor.

Behavioural objectives usually start with some form of standard statement, such as: "By the end of the learning activity, the learner will be competent to:

- list the five stages for completing the company billing process;
- describe the purpose and result of each process stage; and
- demonstrate the complete billing process for three given examples."

Objectives are focusing the attention on the empowered learner and encouraging his/her commitment. A specific learning (or "behavioural") objective will also give the champion some indication of the standards against which s/he must assess performance, in order to judge when the learner has achieved that particular objective.

In the example, you'll notice that each statement has a different activity –

- List
- Describe
- Demonstrate

These action verbs give a strong indication of the activity which the learner will be involved in achieving. This in turn gives indications of the types of techniques which the workplace champion can use to check understanding. Thus, taking learning objectives at a slightly less formal level, if champions can be encouraged to at least think objectively in this way, they'll be beginning to establish the foundations for designing championing sessions. Please take a moment to consider the benefits of applying objective thinking in this way. We will consider learning objectives in much greater detail in the following chapter.

This technique of specifying both a learning activity and an end point objectively is therefore a very valuable tool to apply in workplace championing. Properly written learning objectives can present many indicators relating to the content, techniques and outcomes for specific learning activities. The learning sequences given as case studies throughout this book illustrate how the champion can progressively think in an objective way, reviewing logical sequences of learning and considering the activities implied by particular action verbs.

7. Applying a range of learning techniques

Example – Interpreting activities from objectives

Earlier in this section, we considered the sequence of –

1. list 2. describe 3. demonstrate

I've just taken delivery of a new satellite set-top box for my TV and am rather confused about how to connect it up. My friend is going to show me how to do it and here are the objective stages he has decided we are going to follow.

1. List the various leads/connectors involved – and the appropriate sockets on the set-top box

This is the type of information which you will often see at the beginning of a manual – with detailed illustrations of the control panel, sockets etc and information regarding the leads and connectors which are supplied or required separately.

We can interpret from the verb "list" that we need to know where they are located on the panel – or check off visually that the actual items are present in the box, without at this stage necessarily being totally aware of what their function is.

So, from this statement, we should be clear of the –

- basic information which is required at this stage;
- the simple "show and tell" method required to illustrate the different components; and
- the importance of getting the information over simply, to provide an overview.

My (champion) friend would therefore indicate the various sockets and connecting leads, then get me to point to or select requested real items identified from the overall list. It's a brief and basic stage in the learning process but nevertheless important, as it ensures that the foundations of knowledge are present and correct.

We would then move directly on to the second stage.

2. Describe the functions of the different sockets, controls and connectors

There may be different schools of thought on the importance of this. Those following the "black box" view of technology might consider that it's not important to know why you're connecting a particular plug to a socket, as long as you match red with red; blue with blue and so on.

For the purpose of the exercise, we'll subscribe to the view that there is a benefit in knowing, for example –

- Why the special Scart lead is used to connect between box and TV.
- That this Scart lead must be inserted in a particular way, to avoid damage.
- The difference between a satellite and terrestrial co-axial plug and socket.
- The sockets which must have connections, with the optional extra functions.

So, at this stage in the learning, my friend (acting as my champion) would explain each of the functions previously briefly overviewed in the "list" stage. He would then ask me to describe particular functions, methods of connection and any particular tips and techniques for ensuring that the set-top box is finally connected fully and correctly. At this stage, notice, I'm describing how to do things – not actually doing them yet.

This is the intermediate, safety check stage, to ensure that I know what I should be doing before I actually do it. Again, it may be quite brief for a simple exercise such as this – but it is important.

It must be acknowledged that some Activists would, by this time, have tried different plugs in different sockets and had a general trial and error session until the box was (potentially) connected and functioning. Although this method might arguably be possible for such a basic (and relatively safe) exercise, reinforcing the logical sequence would be very important for parallel procedures such as the safe operation of a lathe or circular saw. Here, there is little scope for experimental error and the company, as training instigator, is governed by Health and Safety requirements for implementing safe procedures in championing as well as more formal responses.

3. Demonstrate the connection and operation of the set-top box

In this final stage, my friend would first show me how the various connections were made – based on the lists and descriptions already covered. He would then disconnect everything and monitor my attempt to demonstrate the operations involved in connecting the set-top box to function properly, with all connections made and checked.

This is a simple example but it serves to illustrate that after inputs from my champion friend at each of the three stages, it's **me**, as learner, who is listing, describing and demonstrating. It is the learner's behaviour which is being developed and assessed by the champion. Bear this in mind as we proceed through the book, considering the different ways of developing or growing the champion's skills and technique.

The champion's awareness of a range of learning techniques

Consider the idiom: "variety is the spice of life".

It's always been the case that teachers and those involved in the development of others have applied a range of techniques to try to maintain as high a level of motivation and on-going interest as possible. Exercises, practical examples, audio visual resources, computer-based (or e-learning) programmes, discussions, group work – as well as face-to-face teaching or lecturing ... the list could run on. There are various models used to identify different preferred styles of learning – and then respond to them with the most appropriate techniques. The outcome generally is that, although the model might identify an overall preferred style of learning for each learner, these same learners will –

- choose to learn using a variety of different methods overall;
- acknowledge that certain types of learning require particular techniques; and
- as a preferred individual learner, still select training course attendance on occasion, for social as well as educational reasons.

In order to best meet these varied requirements, current best practice combines different techniques in a mix that satisfies the learning needs as closely as possible. Where this can be targeted at individual learner level and preferences (as is the case when planning workplace championing responses), the selected techniques and resources should ensure that the resultant learning is as effective as possible. This combination of various techniques and resources is referred to as blended learning.

Blended learning

This combination or integration of techniques requires detailed thought – so we'll only introduce the general concept here. It will be applied progressively in several case studies later in the book.

The important elements of blended learning to note at our championing level are:

- individual needs, levels and preferences should be taken into account;
- self-study materials can be considered where appropriate (for foundation, theoretical study, for example), to relieve time involvement by the champion; and
- clear, stated objectives (or outcomes) for the different events and resources will help us select a blended programme in a structured, progressive way.

Champions can respond to these elements by being –

- aware of the learning preferences of particular learners;
- informed about the required outcomes of the championing sessions;
- involved in planning the overall resource and delivery design; and
- clear about practical workplace applications to reinforce the learning.

Applied workplace championing

For those training to be full-time trainers, this study of different learning styles and techniques can become quite complex. At workplace championing level, we need to keep the detail in perspective. Certainly, the champion should be aware that there is a range of techniques. S/he should also be aware that different learners will prefer various communication methods, in line with preferred learning styles. Both should be taken into consideration when one-to-one learning events are being designed.

Although we briefly cover various aspects of learning styles and techniques throughout this book, this is one area where developing champions may require additional assistance from the DSF (and especially the training department). The champion will benefit from discussing the possibilities of particular resources and techniques with more experienced champions and trainers, in order to better understand the selection process involved. There may even be a benefit in providing specific overview workshops for developing champions, to consider the applications of the overall range available.

Responding to preferred championing styles

Remember, we're hoping to involve as many people as possible in these workplace championing activities. At the early stages where individual champions are becoming tentatively involved in championing activities, it's likely that they will be more confident using some techniques than others. Early success in these first championing activities is important, so they should be encouraged to initially focus on techniques which they feel comfortable using. As their confidence grows, they can gradually incorporate a wider range, with assistance as required.

For example, our embryo champion may not be confident using computer screens but may be happy talking through steps and stages with the aid of hand-drawn diagrams. Using "ad-hoc" sketches is initially fine.

Again, many people are uneasy with public speaking to large groups and might never be capable of talking coherently to a group of mixed trainees. They might, however, be quite confident when talking informally to one learner, while demonstrating a particularly familiar operation. You may thus have to reassure any fears that championing may involve formal training presentation.

Champions should become initially involved through applying whichever delivery skills they feel confident using. In time, after discussing and applying the benefits of computer-based learning, they may move from hand-drawn diagram to Powerpoint™ illustration, if this is considered important. Remember our child-analogy of learning, progressing gradually from crawling to walking to running. When champions are being developed, they should be allowed to walk confidently before being encouraged to start running!

8. The importance of consolidation in the learning process

Many learners have difficulty in recalling the detail of a formal training event after a few days. This problem is often heightened where the learner doesn't get a proper, overseen opportunity to put his/her new learning into practice back in the workplace. The trainer on the formal course is rarely available for post-course discussions and remedial inputs and the on-site help from line managers is, at best, variable. The learner may attempt to apply some of the ideas but, where difficulties are encountered and not resolved, s/he may be tempted to revert to former methods.

This is where the many real benefits of workplace championing can be applied –

- it's exactly that – workplace based;
- the trainee learns it in the workplace, on-site;
- the champion is experienced in the particular activities which will be practised;
- the learning is relevant to the specific department's methods and practices;
- both parties can arrange for practical consolidation to happen, post-learning;
- these consolidation exercises will happen relevantly in the workplace;
- using the department's own facilities, the activities will be directly relevant;
- supporting activities can be arranged rapidly to meet specific learning needs;
- the champion is more likely to be available at short notice to help remedially; and
- as widespread championing evolves, a co-operative atmosphere grows.

It's very cost-effective as well – which makes the finance department happy!

This all-important consolidation of the initial learning input comes both through these related, on-going practical experiences in the workplace and through being able to call on additional, ad-hoc support from the champion "buddy".

The key benefit is probably this availability.

- The champion is available, in all probability working close to the learner, and is therefore on-hand to give additional brief inputs. These will assist the learner over any blockages which may occur, when s/he tries to apply the new ideas.
- The department's own equipment and facilities will be available for use during consolidating practical exercises, so the reinforcement will be more relevant than using generalised case studies/exercises on a public training course.
- The learning time off-the-job will be more available as well, where managers and supervisors are supporting the integrated triangle concept co-operatively.

- Specific solutions are more available to meet individual needs, through the dynamic combination of learner, champion and development support activities and resources.

9. Champions must be capable of setting up reinforcement exercises

Practical exercises must reinforce each individual's learning – the exercises you find in commercially produced programmes are sometimes not specific enough to satisfy particular business needs. The champion must be able to identify and highlight the learning points which he is asking the learner to reinforce through practice. The degree of success is dependent on the objective thinking process we've been considering. If the champion's clear about the message which is being given to the learner, it's easier to establish *exactly* how this must be reinforced practically.

As a champion, where you have to select strategies to explain the connection between the information and the exercise, be as clear as possible about your required outcome – and select materials and activities that meet it as closely as possible. There's a temptation to use facilities or resources that are already available. Reading the title of a book or resources pack is not enough – the champion must check the objectives and detail to make sure that the content reinforces their intended learning message correctly and in enough detail. If the package doesn't have stated objectives/outcomes – or these are couched in general terms such as "show an enhanced awareness of ....", consider its potential use very carefully.

Through selecting these resources consciously (and adding any extra information which may be lacking), it should be relatively easy to set up totally relevant work experiences within the department where both the champion and learner work. The facilities and/or equipment are there, the conditions are obviously exactly as they are in real working life (as compared to some simulated exercise in a training department) and the implications of any restrictions (staff, physical, financial or resource) become naturally factored into the exercise, based on inside knowledge.

The learning environment is therefore as relevant and significant as possible. In terms of learning interactions, we are creating a fairly perfect workplace CPD (continuing professional development) environment, where a range of developed champions can service a wide variety of development needs. This is supported by an overall system which has been set up to respond to these needs rapidly and effectively. A championing system obviously takes time to evolve but the wide-ranging results are certainly well worth the effort.

Focus Time 3.3 – Case Study

Greg has recently become chairman of the works council. He's been a member of one or two committees in the past and showed great enthusiasm to get involved in the works council – but has never been a chairman before. His first meeting functioning as chairman was not controlled very successfully, with people arguing with each other across the table, irrelevant issues being discussed in great depth – and the meeting over-running by the best part of an hour. There was also a lack of decisions and outcomes being reached.

David is a senior manager in the company, six years away from retiring and with a wealth of experience at chairing various committees over the years. He sits in on the works council to represent management but has not been chairman of this, as the company policy is that the chair role must come from the direct workforce.

When the minutes of the meeting are produced, there are several comments both from within the works council itself and from one or two senior managers, that there has been a lack of action closure at the meeting, causing unrest, with particular issues dragging on without resolution.

David and Greg meet in the corridor and Greg asks David for his advice on how best to tighten up these works council meetings.

David's suggestions

The immediate problem David identified was that Greg as chairman didn't progress the discussions to particular outcomes or identify enough follow-on actions. However, he suggested that these and other problems are largely due to Greg's lack of awareness of the meeting structures he should be following. He suggested that Greg also needs to be more informed about the expected role of the chairman in helping the group to reach and record decisions before moving on to new issues. It's thus a case of being able to –

- control the meeting members with a light touch;
- be clear about the anticipated outcomes from each discussion topic;
- summarise progress to keep things moving forward; and
- identify an end point and follow-on actions (with responsibilities) for each item.

Suggestions for Greg's CPD

David proposed that Greg should consider some of the following as areas for development. They discussed how the information might either be achieved by attending a course on chairmanship skills – or by talking to internal champions who were identified as being good at committee chairmanship.

David's suggestions for Greg's development areas included –

- some study about the roles and responsibilities of a chairperson;
- identification of the importance of closing agenda items before progressing;
- observing an effective chairperson in action – focus on controlling discussion;
- consideration of time management and prioritisation, for effective meetings; and
- review how the agenda can be used to keep discussion under control.

Some people, such as David, have "development skills in their genes" and tend to be able to spot opportunities for practical reinforcement. They're happy to explain or demonstrate good practice to someone else who displays an interest. This is a trait which we're on the look out for when selecting our first "natural born champions". Others can develop these skills, given a little extra help and encouragement.

10. Champions must be aware how their specialist subjects relate to others

There's a lot of talk nowadays about "Seeing the bigger picture". In this case, the bigger picture represents the inter-relationships of subjects and departments and the impact which these will have upon each other. There are people who are totally caught up with the detail of their own particular specialities and show little awareness – or even concern – about the priorities of others. We need to develop a wider awareness in our workplace champions, to encourage the holistic growth of these coaching, mentoring and informal tutoring activities across the business. We can begin to do this through –

- increased awareness through inter-departmental meetings and communications;
- encouraging people to consider the knock-on effects of proposed actions;
- applied lateral thinking, to assess the outcomes resulting from different inputs;
- ensuring that people remain informed – and that the detail is accurate; and
- discussing the relationships between different departments and the overall production of the key products/outcomes of the business.

Growing Champions holistically

There's that "H" word again! Remember, with the holistic approach, we're trying to combine different individual actions together positively, so that we achieve a bonus, add-on result. In workplace championing, this improves where the champions are aware of each other, what they are doing as a team and how their particular skills can combine, interweave and complement each other. A champion, for example, could be aware that a suitable practical experience – which might be harder for him to set up – is readily available in another department. He could then arrange for his learner to experience this in the other department, perhaps offering to reciprocate in some way in the future.

Thinking back to our works council example, there might be a very effectively run committee in another department that we could arrange for Greg to sit in and observe, with a list of particular learning points to look out for. He could then make notes for further discussions with David.

There are lots of other possibilities, if you think through some of your own priorities.

So, these are ten of the key characteristics that your organisation should be trying to develop, when identifying and growing the team of workplace champions.

Just think - you could be one of them!

Techniques for championing

Because we're applying an integrated approach, our study so far has been thinking of any particular person as being a champion – but also at other times becoming the learner. In a support role, the same individual could at times even be involved in helping organise the development of others. This is the nature of the co-operative integration which the model generates – but it does make the overall picture more complicated. Keep the image of the integrated triangle clearly in your mind. This will help you to understand the inter-relationships and see how different roles can co-exist.

So, at times, you'll be calling on others as champions – on-site specialist help which you might request when wanting to learn some new skill. On these occasions, you'll assume the role of individual learner, while still remaining "on call" as a champion

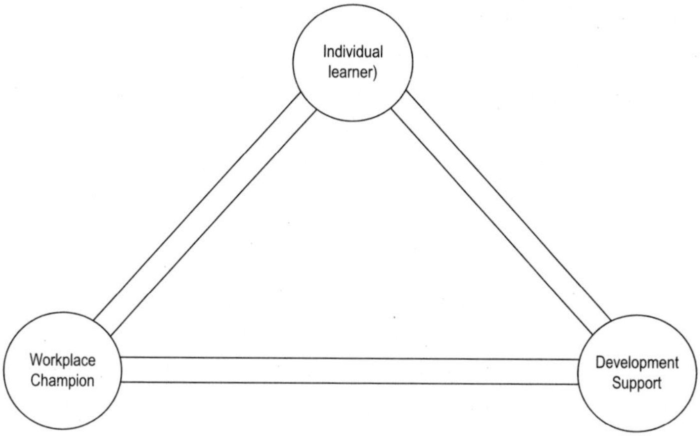

for your identified specific learning areas. If you're also a manager, supervisor or member of the other development support functions we've identified, you might also be involved as a support member, helping to build the whole programme.

This is all part of the overall plan. If the foundations and support are in place, virtually everyone can get involved to some degree in both championing others and being championed themselves. Building the model certainly takes time – and some people will be less involved than others. Also, some percentage of these people will take more than they give back to the system ... but life isn't perfect. So, though we're primarily concerned with the techniques of how to grow workplace champions, as the book title states, this is only part of the overali process of setting up a complete strategy. We can be involved in many facets, simultaneously.

Keep thinking laterally – retain that image of the integrated triangle.

Imagine, as it begins to revolve, how the three different roles begin to blend together, as the co-operative atmosphere grows.

Focus 3.4 – A reality check

Perhaps there's the need for a little injection of reality here. Although a picture's evolving where everyone's potentially getting involved in the workplace champion process, that doesn't mean they're all rushing around madly coaching and mentoring each other for a large percentage of their working lives, with little conventional work being done. If the atmosphere and resources are right, much of the developmental activity can happen in very short response bursts – clearing up a blockage and getting the individual learner operational again.

Any single individual only requires limited development over a given time, so the overall time requirements involved in championing activities needn't become unrealistic. The overwhelming benefit, however, is the wide range of input available to really address individual problems in a SMART and SERIOUS way.

Just think of the scope for this individual, focused CPD happening in an informal but organised way throughout an organisation. Think of the improved communication and the more bonded inter-relationships between individuals and departments. If the foundations are right, think of the consistent atmosphere of co-operation which can be developed. That's the holistic effect. Can you buy into the idea?

Focus 3.5 – The Workplace Champion

So, we've established that there are various traits and skills which build towards helping someone become a workplace champion. Many of these may occur naturally in some of us or might require a degree of initial input to start us off. We've also identified that we're not looking for a fully proficient teacher or public speaker when we're encouraging someone to get involved in this championing. Let's spend a moment considering the differences.

It's more than likely that you have experienced the skills of a professional trainer – and perhaps also some form of public speaker. You've certainly experienced a full range of teachers, although memories of these might be in the fairly distant past!

When training a trainer or public speaker, there are various areas which we cover. Some are specific to the fact that the individual has to, in effect, perform in front of an audience. These might include the ability to:

- project the voice;
- use visual aids effectively;
- appear confident;
- develop rapport with and amongst the audience;
- ensure that mannerisms do not distract; and
- use the "stage" to best effect (such as not standing rigidly on the spot).

These are of less importance when developing workplace championing skills.

Key criteria for effective championing

There are however other training/public speaking criteria, concerned with getting the message across, which are as important for effective championing as they are for more formal training.

These will include the ability to:

- structure the message with a beginning, middle and end – an introduction, main development and consolidation;
- use language that the learner understands;
- recap at regular intervals, to allow the new information to be consolidated;
- present examples which are relevant to both the workplace and the learner;
- build the information progressively, through a sequence of sub-objectives; and
- identify the pace of learning which will best suit the learner(s).

Workplace champions thus don't have to be grand performers or public speakers. Championing, being primarily a one-to-one activity, can go on quietly in a corner somewhere, with little flourish or glitz. It does however require planning, structure, objective thinking and correct pace in order to succeed. We will be considering how to achieve these competencies throughout the remainder of this book.

Meeting workplace needs

A key benefit of championing is the fact that it functions directly within the workplace that it's serving. This must result in a stronger guarantee that the learning and development which is taking place is directly relevant to the needs of that workplace and the individuals working there.

Focus 3.6 – Workplace development priorities

These priorities include the importance of –

- *the learning matching the needs and priorities of the workplace;*
- *development sessions fitting in with existing time peaks and troughs;*
- *each learner being clear of his/her learning objectives/outcomes;*
- *each champion being aware of basic techniques for structuring input;*
- *each champion being seen as competent in the selected subject/skill;*
- *the champion arranging relevant practical reinforcement exercises;*
- *an agreement "contract" being in place for the championing relationship;*
- *the background organisation being in place to match participants;*
- *the overall monitoring of the effectiveness of the programme; and*
- *agreed resources and practical support being available as required.*

Much of this can be organised at departmental or group level – although some of the people organisation and management overview responsibilities are better achieved at a company-wide level, arranged by HR and Training. This allows for an improved "bigger picture" overview, with a blending of techniques and personnel where appropriate, making the whole workplace championing programme as cost- and time-effective as possible. It takes time to prepare the foundations and guidelines but, once established – and as long as support remains consistent – the integrated workplace championing model can grow exponentially.

4 Thinking Objectively

One-minute overview

This chapter examines how to use objective thinking to focus the structure and expected outcomes of learning within our workplace championing model. The importance of individual learner involvement and empowerment is emphasised through his/her description as an "empowered learner". Through use of examples, we consider the structure and content represented by learning objectives – and how these can indicate sequence, learning progressions, preferred styles and the milestone results of our championing events. This chapter also explores the relationship between specified objectives, individual competency levels and the function of benchmarking. Finally, it reviews the importance of applying and responding to a range of learning styles, to ensure the most effective results.

Terminology

We've played around with a variety of related words so far –

- outcomes
- outputs
- goals
- aims
- objectives
- sequenced steps
- bite-sized chunks

– to name but a few.

Although they all mean slightly different things, we're not about to spend the rest of the chapter researching the definitions and differences! What we are concerned about is that the concept behind them all relates to focus.

- The clearer you are about where you're going, the easier it will be to keep moving forward in the right direction.
- The clearer our learner is about the final milestone, goal, objective etc, the surer they will be that they have finally reached it.
- The more the champion and learner can focus on the stages along the way – the milestones – the more direct the learning path will be.
- The clearer you are about the sequence of information necessary to advance between these milestones, the easier the progress will be.
- The more precise the practical consolidation exercises are, the better – and longer – the new information will be retained.

Another phrase which we've used several times so far is "thinking bigger picture". This is another important element of our objective approach. Bigger picture thinking occurs, for example, where we consider the implications behind various outcomes, then actively review the range of options open to us before selecting the way which is best overall.

Learning Objectives

Learning objectives focus first and foremost on what the individual learner will be competent to do by the end of the learning event. To state these as clearly as possible, we should always think of the statements as action phrases, starting with a verb or action which we will expect our learner to be able to do.

In order to be even clearer, we should also include some precise standards.

Focus Time 4.1

So, for *example, if we were wanting to write a learning objective for producing a simple PowerPoint™ presentation, we might write the objective as:*

By the end of the learning event, the learner will be competent in – producing a sequence of five screens incorporating clear and brief bullet point phrases from given subject statements, using a consistent screen style throughout and applying at least two visual techniques to introduce new text statements to particular screens.

Look closely at the statement for a moment. In terms of planning how we'll assess that the learner is finally competent, what do we have to check? Here's a list:

- the information must progress over at least five screens;
- the information must be presented clearly, probably in bullet points;
- the screens must show a consistent "house style"; and
- at least two techniques for "flying in" information must be used.

Each of these is an action (or actions) which the learner must achieve. Some actions are to do with designing the actual wording of the presentation – others are purely focusing on the operation of the PowerPoint™ programme. Both design and operation must be achieved for this particular objective to be satisfied.

However, this objective could subdivide further – one action is the design of the content detail, while the other involves producing the short PowerPoint™ presentation. It all depends on how we want to focus on the learner's progress and outcome achievements. That's what precise objectives are all about.

Establishing prior competence

Let's say we have an empowered learner who has already had experience of designing information in a clear, logical sequence. She could prove her design competence by showing examples of work she has already planned and used. If this is assessed as OK (that is, she has proved her competency), she can move straight to learning about the technicalities of PowerPoint™ production.

In our type of learning situation, she would know that she was OK on the content design – therefore the development need would rapidly focus on actually producing the PowerPoint™ presentation. In the initial discussion between champion and individual learner, they would sort out specifically what their objective was, giving the champion more detailed indications of the final blended activities he might select.

To summarise so far, thinking in an objective way can help us:

- plan the content of our learning/championing session;
- establish the starting point/previous competency of our learner;
- identify the key steps and stages leading to achieving the objective; and
- select indicators to assess that the learner has achieved the objective.

Taking it a stage further, thinking objectively will also give indicators which help us:

- consider the best technique to use to formulate the information;
- select activities which reinforce the learning effectively; and
- position a particular learning event alongside other related events.

Action Time 4.1

Think of some activity which you would like to learn how to do. This section will give the steps and stages of an example. You may find it useful to develop your own parallel example as we progress and make notes of it separately.

1. **General activity.**
   – Learn how to make a leek and cheese sauce flan.
2. **Component elements.**
   - how to make/prepare pastry
   - how to prepare the leeks
   - how to produce the cheese sauce
   - the overall cooking steps and stages
3. **Selection of competency shortfall area(s).**
   I am going to use frozen, ready-made pastry, so don't need to know how to make pastry; I have sautéed leeks and other vegetables before when making soup, so that's OK. I have a recipe which tells me the stages of part pre-baking the flan case, adding the sautéed leeks, covering this with the cheese sauce for final cooking etc – but it assumes I know how to make a cheese sauce. I don't.
   My development need therefore is to learn how to make a cheese sauce.
4. **Specific, objective statement of what I need to achieve, as empowered learner.**
   I need to become competent at producing a lump-free cheese sauce, in the correct volume to use for a vegetable (in this case leek) flan to serve four people (22 cm dish). (NOTICE: This is an objective statement stated in a fairly user-friendly way!)
5. **Champion's initial ideas about how to achieve this outcome.**
   - Talk about skills involved (adding flour gradually to melted butter, then milk – while stirring to make sure that there are no lumps etc).
   - Identify ingredients and amounts required for 22 cm flan dish sized meal.
   - Demonstrate mixing and preparation with a small volume of sauce.
   - Supervise individual learner mixing and preparing small volume of sauce.

6. **Consideration of facilities and resources necessary to carry out the activity.** (Kitchen facilities, including stove [oven not necessary as this is purely a sauce-making exercise]; ample quantities of all ingredients; kitchen equipment (flan dish etc.)

If you've thought through a parallel example of your own, spend a moment or two before proceeding to check that you've included enough information and that you've covered the various areas included in the above example.

Holistic combinations

You'll note that this is a joint effort – some of the detail comes from the workplace champion while other details are focused on the individual learner. That's fine because it's really the activity we're building here, with the learner and workplace champion co-operating to reach the outcome. Notice that the individual learner is actively involved in making the exercise as relevant to his needs as possible – the championing model refers to him as an "empowered learner" in order to underline this active involvement.

You should also notice that thinking in an objective way has helped us to get a clear picture, not only about the actual specific learning activity which is involved but also:

- where the development need fits into the overall activity;
- what other competencies are involved;
- the possible learning techniques which can be used;
- the resources which are required; and
- the standards which can be used to check the learner's competency.

So, thinking objectively really helps to focus our thoughts, in many different ways.

Learning progressions

This is another area where clear learning objectives can help greatly.

Sorting out a learning progression is basically figuring out a logical sequence of building blocks. Doing this will gradually construct a solid, join-free knowledge and understanding. There is of course a difference between information and knowledge. With access to the internet, among other sources, we can all become information-saturated. Applying it in a knowledgeable way is a different (and higher) rung of the ladder. This is where the three "C"s from our previous list –

- Conversant
- Credible
- Creative

– come into play.

We need to be both informed about the information and capable of applying it in a knowledgeable way; we need to be seen and acknowledged by others as capable of using the knowledge confidently and openly – and we need to be capable of using the knowledge in parallel and new ways ... by "thinking outside the box".

Learning objectives

We need to get our basics firmly established before we can confidently push against the outer perimeters. In the previous chapter, we cited a sequence of active learning steps as:

- List
- Describe
- Demonstrate

This illustrates the three initial stages of learning development, upon which the integrated triangle concept is built. These are –

- Knowledge
- Comprehension
- Application.

In factual areas, this gives the behaviour stages as –

- learn any new terminology and get it right;
- understand how the terminology actually applies; and
- perform exercises applying and reinforcing it.

In practical areas (such as our cheese sauce example – Section 5), this means:

- talk through the components and skills involved;
- see the skills demonstrated slowly and precisely; and
- perform the exercise carefully, under supervision.

So, thinking objectively gives us a logical sequence to follow for any activity. The structuring involved is based on what is termed "behaviourist" thinking. This states that learning will be most effective if you initially know the theoretical background of how to do something. Once these foundation steps are in place, the learner should then become comfortable with the concepts, words and techniques used. Then, and only then, is it considered appropriate that the learner finally attempts the activity under supervision. This is (very basically) the behaviourist approach upon which the workplace championing model is constructed – there are of course alternative schools of thought, which we do not intend to explore here.

Going back to "thinking bigger picture" again, objective planning also helps us to see the logical steps and stages when there is a larger learning activity involved.

Focus Time 4.2

Keep thinking Knowledge, Comprehension and Application but, instead of a short exercise like making a cheese sauce, think of a longer progression of learning – like learning to drive, for example. We considered the importance of having a sequence of outcomes earlier. Now we can combine this with our awareness of development sequences, in order to see how theoretical and practical elements combine.

For example, you need to know –

- Initially, where the main controls (clutch, accelerator etc) are – and what each one does – before your first attempt to make the car move.
- The basic principle of going round roundabouts – and understand the positioning in correct lanes – before you actually drive out onto your first roundabout (and when you do, make it a small, easy one!).
- What the main signs in the Highway Code are – and what they mean – before you can respond to them out on the road.
- The effects of turning your steering wheel while moving in reverse – and how you can change angles dramatically when reversing into a traffic coned space – before your first attempt at reversing to park in the space between two cars at the side of the road.
- The rules and priorities for turning right from a major road – to allow you to take up the correct position on the crown of the road – before making your first attempt on a busy road.

We could go on but these examples underline the principle – know the terminology and basic theory first – then go through the detailed steps and stages of the process (having first watched someone else demonstrate) and then, thirdly, apply your learning through practical experience.

Getting the Sequence Right

Thinking through the same driving example in an objective way, you'll also see that certain learning steps come before others. This is another benefit of thinking logically – or applying objective sequences. It may appear like common sense – if it does, this implies that you think in a logical, objective way normally, which is good. Thinking like this should make your job, of planning workplace championing events and selecting the best sequence of learning, a lot easier.

Try thinking even "bigger picture". We've progressed from using objective thinking to make a cheese sauce, to applying it for single activities such as reversing a car into a roadside space or turning right on a major road. Now think about its application in the overall planning of how you might teach someone to drive. In order to see the overall sequence, let's think along the lines of:

- Initially, you need to go through some of the basic theory.
- Then you might go with the learner driver to a deserted car park and practice the basic control and steering operations.
- Next you might take the learner driver to a quiet road, demonstrate the basic actions of road using, and then let him drive. Initially you would keep well away from roundabouts, traffic lights etc.
- When you were confident that s/he could start, stop, steer and basically manoeuvre the car in quiet traffic, you could explain the theory of traffic lights, roundabouts etc (doing this in stages).

- Then, when out on the road, you would brief him/her on what to do before s/he actually approached each hazard. Initially talking him/her through the operation would make sure that s/he subsequently achieved it successfully.
- Progressively, you would give fewer prompts – only correcting actions as necessary. This is gradually empowering him/her to make the decisions and take more responsibility for driving the car.
- As the learner driver's confidence grew, you would gradually involve him/her in more complicated situations (multi-lane roundabouts, turning right on busy roads, parking in tighter spaces etc). At each new experience, you would brief him/her first – then prompt as necessary to help him/her succeed.

Progressively, as the learner gains confidence, the driving instructor would be saying less and less, merely making suggestions or correcting errors of judgement periodically, to underline the learning. It's likely you've experienced the process of learning how to drive and you may also have sat alongside a learner driver, coaching them while they gain some practical experience on the road. If this is the case, you should recognise some of the steps and stages described here – and will also appreciate the progressive sequences involved in changing ideas into practice.

Action Time 4.2

Assuming that you are an experienced driver, think of one or two elements of driving which you found relatively difficult to learn. Try to identify the particular manoeuvres, complex detail or relationships with other road-users which made these particular elements difficult for you.

With the benefit of experience, can you think of activities or inputs which you could have experienced, which would have helped you overcome those particular blockages?

Example

Let's focus on reversing, which involves the techniques of –

- using mirrors;
- looking backwards over each shoulder;
- being aware of "blind spots" in particular vehicles;
- experiencing the heightened effects of turning the steering wheel;
- judging kerb positioning, both nearside and offside;
- locating the rear bumper position when reversing towards a solid object; and
- developing the special co-ordination of feet actions when travelling in reverse.

Where any particular element is identified as being especially difficult, it should be isolated and particular exercises devised to give supervised coaching and practice.

This is an example of building a framework upon which learning needs analysis and objectives development are constructed.

If you don't drive, you may benefit from talking to a driver to consolidate the detail above – or you may be able to construct a parallel example.

Competencies and Benchmarks

It's likely that you've come across these two current "buzzwords". Used correctly, they both involve objective thinking.

Competency

If someone is competent at doing something, they have achieved an agreed standard for carrying out an action or series of actions. That's virtually identical to our definition for the achievement of an objective. Perhaps the additional secret ingredient which makes an achieved objective into a competency is the extra experience or consolidation. Competency usually indicates a broader capability than merely being able to achieve an objective (which could be represented by a one-off activity). You would expect someone who was competent at a particular task to complete it confidently and smoothly, without "joins" or steps and stages showing.

Going back to our driving example, the individual learner could be at the stage where she can consistently use the controls to drive off and change gear smoothly. However, she may still panic and stall the car if put in a more stressful situation. At this stage, she's achieved the objective of operating the foot controls to drive consistently, using the full range of gears.

Consolidation

We could say that her competency is still below acceptable levels until she's had enough experience to allow her to change gear and maintain control of the engine without consciously thinking about it – or in emergency situations. This should come through practical experience, often referred to as the "consolidation". It's important, of course, that this consolidation reinforces the standards which were set during the earlier stages of learning. Remember our points relating to Nellie earlier!

This is one of the most important tenets of being a mentor, coach, trainer, teacher or anyone bringing new learning experience to another – being responsible for the consistent reinforcement of acceptable standards. In other words, this involves ensuring that learners remain competent within the current workplace requirements.

This is where benchmarking helps.

Benchmarking

This involves setting points of reference – presenting a range of consistent standards which people can then aspire to achieve. How are these standards established? By identifying the "best practice" applied by key players in the particular field of business. It will be carried out scientifically, of course, taking in a wide enough spread to be mathematically significant – and will also include reference to any nationally accepted standards.

So, from our position of thinking objectively in order to meet particular standards, it'll be easier to establish our objectives if we have sets of standards already in existence through benchmarking. Remember that they're a reference point however – we could decide that our particular objective had a standard which was higher (or lower) than the benchmarked standard.

A benchmark was originally a mark cut in stone by surveyors to indicate a point in a consistent line of levels. Once there, it's fixed. Equally, our standard, once established, would be fixed as far as our different learners are concerned. Any situation where the goal posts are shifted makes it confusing for all concerned. Writing down the objective, with standards, is marking our outcome "in stone".

We should be aware, however, that benchmarking is creating an "average", in the sense that it may become the general target towards which companies and individuals will be aiming. By definition, the more individuals we have proudly achieving the quality benchmarked standard, the greater the number of like (or similar) performers we're amassing. Taking this to the extreme, we're tending towards the "cloning" of carbon-copy practitioners! At one and the same time, we're encouraging the meeting of acceptable standards but also potentially discouraging the individual, entrepreneurial striving for additional aspects. In relation to the seven "C"s we reviewed earlier, we're focusing on the Consistency without allowing for the Creativity. There is, in short, a limiting aspect to benchmarking and quality assurance, if we're looking from the "big picture", entrepreneurial viewpoint. It does however provide a clear initial reference point on which to focus.

Objectives – a review of progress

However you go about it, and whatever stage you are at when you apply these objective thinking ideas, we suggest you return to this chapter periodically to refresh your focus on applying objectives. It's a particular way of thinking where, the more you use and apply the encapsulated ideas, the more you'll appreciate the guidelines and prompts which objective thinking provides.

Focus Time 4.3
A personal Case Study

I worked with my first "objectives mentor" when I started lecturing in a Further Education College in London. Prior to this, I'd taught for several years in the early 70s, without really being aware of learning objectives very much at all. It must have taken about seven years of tentative application and several different experiences working in the fields of education and business development before I became competent enough to use them flexibly. By then, I had progressed from merely reproducing the theory and structures to being confident enough to actually apply objective thinking proactively to meet a range of experiences. I was applying it as a valuable tool, rather than using it as an academic exercise in its own right. It did take seven years, however!

By this stage in my career, I was largely involved in the design of customised business training programmes and the scripting and production of open learning and interactive video learning materials. These activities underlined to me that thinking objectively took me further than merely establishing outcomes and standards – to a level which also provided indicators of most appropriate delivery techniques, best practical reinforcement activities and "target population" expectations of learner competency at the various stages of development. It was only then that I began to really appreciate the breadth of applications possible, allowing my own Creativity to kick in. I'm now passionate about the really valuable assistance that objective thinking can bring to getting championing kick-started – but it does take time to learn and apply confidently.

Using objectives may seem slightly laborious initially but do keep persevering with them in any situations where they seem appropriate. Similarly, thinking in an objective way helps you plan ahead and clarify your goals, as well as encouraging a logical, sequential way of thinking. It's encouraging the left brain foundation builder to provide the confident basis on which your right brain creativity can then sprout wings and fly! Use both left and right hemispheres for the most dynamic results.

The major benefits of using the full range of objective thinking in the worlds of learning development and applied workplace championing are that we receive –

- a clearer awareness of what the session is attempting to achieve;
- help in identifying the key learning points precisely;
- ideas about how the learning session should progress logically;
- indicators of the learning stages which need reinforcement and checking; and
- decisions regarding the best techniques for getting the message across.

Objective thinking and learning styles

There is a wide range of ways of learning – different ways suit different people and some techniques will be most appropriate for learning specific subject areas. There's no single answer to any learning question, however, so responses to individual learning requirements must remain flexible. Think of yourself – do you always learn best using the same technique, or do you (like many) find that "variety is the spice of life"? Are there times when you prefer learning on a course, as part of a group where you can discuss ideas – whereas, for some other more factual subjects, you find using a good text book or interactive programme (such as open or e-learning) to be the best option?

There are many different theories relating to learning styles – key the two words into your computer search engine and you'll have a choice of well over nineteen million results, so we're not going to cover the different options here! You'll be aware of your own preferred styles, whatever fancy titles they might answer to, and be able to relate these to particular areas of learning. The key thing to remember, as a workplace champion, is that each individual learner with whom you're working will also have preferred and flexible learning styles. These may vary to some degree between individual learners – and may also differ from your own preferences.

As a workplace champion, if you're trying to make the learning experience relevant to each individual, make sure you respond to his or her preferences as much as you can when planning your championing activity. How do you establish these preferences? Ask, listen and discuss – it's all about communication!

Focus Time 4.4
A practical example

With some subjects, the learner can absorb the factual foundations (that's the Knowledge and Understanding stages) on their own using a structured learning programme such as e-learning. A supplementary face-to-face practical session would, in all probability, be required to apply and practise the learning. You can't fully learn a practical skill by using theoretical methods.

So, as a champion, you may expect your empowered learner to have already completed the basic learning from a text book or learning programme before you meet for the follow-up discussion and practical sessions.

Possible problem area

When they finally meet therefore, the champion will be relying on the empowered learner having studied the theory prior to attending. If s/he hasn't, for whatever reason, s/he will be at a disadvantage – and any learning will be slower. The champion may justifiably feel that s/he doesn't have the time to spend going over these basics – the same is true when running a formal training event, where the course delegates have been given "study reading" to complete prior to the course. Any form of learning involvement which relies on individual effort prior to the main learning event requires an empowered learner and clear direction.

This is why we're emphasising the importance of individuals grasping the initiative in our champion model by also referring to the individual learner as the "empowered learner". Focus – empowerment – activation!

The clear direction – and the specification of learning which identifies the necessary foundations, followed by the sequence of different building bricks – is underpinned by the objective way of thinking which we have been considering in this chapter.

Applied variety

The key issue is to realise that there are various learning techniques which can be used. As a champion, don't fall into the rut of using only a very limited repertoire. Even at the more formal level, where training courses may be the organisation's preferred way of learning, trainers are expected to use a variety of methods within the course. These could include individual and group exercises, discussions, worksheets and hands-on practical sessions, to break the monotony of merely talking at the delegates all the time.

The need for variety is even truer for workplace championing, which we are considering to be a more practical activity anyway, generally done on a one-to-one basis. Certainly, maintain an awareness of your individual learner(s) – some will be happier discussing things, while others might prefer to have a worksheet or text book and figure it out for themselves. The additional consciousness that you, as champion, are around to answer queries and get any blockages unstuck, is an incredibly valuable added bonus. Try to respond to it as openly as you can.

Objective focus

Planning your development session objectively will help you identify the types of resources that you'll require. Be as precise as possible. If you're looking for a visual aid which shows the key components in an exploded diagram, for example, that's what you need. Any more generalised, external images of the equipment without specific detail, which the resource provider might well offer instead, will not be suitable. Be clear what you need – and specify this need in detail to those supporting you. It's down to effective communication again.

Objectives and the champion

Objectives encourage precision and focus.

- They're there to help you – don't get bogged down in writing them.
- Consider them as a way of thinking, not a control mechanism.
- Use them to give a structure and sequence to your plans.
- Look for indications of supporting resources and practical exercises.
- They'll help you focus on how your individual learner is progressing.
- They'll indicate when s/he's reached the end point.
- They will help to identify the consolidation milestones along the way.

The way ahead

Remember – the clearer you are of your destination, the more positive your journey will be.

Thinking objectively helps you focus on the destination or outcome – and allows you to identify the steps and stages along the way. It takes time to develop – and it requires on-going refinement. Keep an open mind and always be ready to revisit your decisions, if things are not progressing as you expected. It may just be that you've left too large an expectation gap between learning milestones, and the individual learner is losing the way.

Find someone who is perhaps a little more competent at objective thinking than you are and ask him/her to champion your progress. Having a reference point will make it much easier for you when you meet these points of confusion, and need to discuss the possible options open. Thinking objectively works wonders – persevere with it!

5 Developing Others

One-minute overview

This chapter considers the range of skills and competencies which workplace champions will find useful. These include areas such as identifying and prioritising learning needs, meeting work/life balance requirements, sub-dividing and sequencing outcomes and including on-going reinforcement and problem solving. It includes a variety of short case studies and check lists which will help both the champion and those involved in his/her development – and looks at many of the practicalities of getting the new workplace champion motivated and involved in the first all-important activities. It concludes with sections on applying varied learning styles, achieving competency levels and monitoring/maintaining standards, with the accent on consistency.

In examining objective thinking and its applications, we've been speaking about teachers and trainers as well as workplace champions. It's now time to concentrate more precisely on the kinds of skills and competencies which are important for our "big picture" range of people wanting to be workplace champions – and how they can apply these to help the development of others, as well as themselves. In trying to spread our net of involvement as wide as possible, we have to think as flexibly as possible.

We've established that –

- structure in delivery is valuable;
- logical sequencing of the steps that make up a skilled activity is important;
- formality is often unnecessary for training;
- communication when training is crucial;
- response to identified gaps in skills and knowledge is key; and
- initial attitude by people within an organisation is more important than aptitude.

Let's now consider how we apply all these in championing others.

Championing skills

In our championing programme, we'll be incorporating as wide a variety of skills that may be utilised in the workplace as possible – applying elements of coaching and mentoring to satisfy our overall need to have champions who can respond flexibly to the different learning and motivational levels which they will meet in individual learners.

These levels can involve learners with different:

- amounts of previous experience;
- levels of previous competency in particular areas of skills;
- degrees of receptiveness to new development;

- levels of ability to identify progressive steps and stages of learning; and
- knowledge-levels of particular company systems and processes.

Remember that traditional coaching was more to do with fine-tuning and developing existing skills, while traditional mentoring involved the imparting of new information.

We've already established that thinking in an objective way can help us formulate sequential actions. Thinking in this logical way will clarify the nature of competencies and establish the "building blocks" necessary to work with individual learners, in order to achieve the required competency levels.

We identified natural traits which we would look for or encourage in champions, such as –

- patience
- logical thinking and
- ability to reinforce information practically.

Key techniques and competencies for workplace champions

To review the main techniques and competencies for workplace champions, these are:

- use of objective thinking to identify and prioritise learners' needs;
- ability to identify a sequence of learning outcomes, in manageable "chunks";
- knowledge of a range of simple techniques which can be used for effective and accelerated learning;
- knowledge of the importance of using practical exercises and other means of reinforcement;
- awareness of possible blocks to learner progress and ability to overcome these;
- knowledge of types and implications of different learning styles;
- knowledge of competency levels and monitoring of their achievement;
- importance of maintaining a positive, motivating work atmosphere;
- knowledge of the company processes and key business objectives; and
- awareness of the key inter-relationships within and between departments.

Putting it in perspective

Remember – our development path here is not heading towards training workplace champions to be accredited trainers. The model is focused on developing people who can (and wish to) pass information and skills to others. Developing workplace champions involves finding ways of building on this natural enthusiasm, to give them structures and support which will make their involvement as easy as possible.

One of our key challenges is to ensure that any structured input we provide is seen by them as helping, rather than hindering, their championing involvement. Experience shows that time spent on planning these structures is more than saved during implementation.

Let's consider each of the areas in turn.

Identifying and prioritising staff development needs

This is one of the key outcomes of thinking in an objective way.

When a manager is involved in identifying staff development needs, s/he's mainly ensuring that there's appropriate cover for all current and future departmental activities. So, if the company works three shifts and it's necessary that a particular skill is represented on each shift, it'll be necessary for a minimum of three operatives to be signed off as competent. Taking holidays and sickness into account, a safer number might be four or five.

In some of the "softer" skills, such as communication or interpersonal skills, it might be considered that all or the majority of staff should meet certain competency levels – in which case the identification here would be more of key skills required by the majority rather than overall numbers of staff needing training.

Meeting certificated standards

Again, legislation will require certain skills and qualifications to be represented in the workforce – which will dictate development needs and the volume of cover. Where the certification of the qualification is the important issue (as with Health and Safety matters), the company has no choice but to use accredited training providers, so a more informal level of workplace championing would not be a viable solution, other than for checking and maintaining internal standards.

Compromising on individual priorities

When identifying needs (through appraisal and other forms of individual review), it's usually part of the manager's brief to try to match business and individual objectives. There will be times where an individual might wish to develop a particular skill as part of his own perceived personal development – where the business has no requirement for this individual to be competent in the skill.

It would be down to the individual and his/her manager to discuss the situation in order to achieve an agreed balance. This is combining needs analysis with work/life balance – to achieve the highest degree of motivation overall for each individual learner. Overall training budgets will dictate the types of formal training which can be funded – but here again, the more flexible championing approach can permit some informal input, if deemed beneficial overall. An individual might, for example, be interested in improving her skills in minutes writing or committee chairmanship for use as a member of some community committee. Although not perhaps a key responsibility within her business existence, it would be fairly easy to justify a spin-off benefit for her involvement in departmental team meetings. The end result of one or two championing sessions will be a more motivated individual, displaying improved competency for her roles both at work and in the community. That is a positive result, overall.

Skills and shortfalls

The key response to individual needs analysis is to establish the crucial skills and knowledge which are necessary for that individual to become – and remain – more than competent at his/her job. The emphasis is increasingly on keeping up to speed with new techniques, legislation and information relating to these key competencies, rather than necessarily broadening the knowledge base. This should be reflected in the individual's plans for continuing professional development.

Our workplace-championing model makes this relatively easy to monitor and respond to positively, for the simple reason that the workplace champion and the individual learner are likely to be working together in the same environment – and probably location. This creates a more pro-active atmosphere than is normally possible with formal training responses – and points to the importance of the champions being kept in the picture regarding future skills-requirements.

Sequencing outcomes

This ability to subdivide and sequence logically is one of the key skills required of a workplace champion – especially as many will be very proficient in the key skills of their jobs. As illustrated in our earlier driving example, this natural, largely unconscious capability may make it difficult for some champions to understand why others have problems in mastering the techniques. We've spoken about the innate patience which many teachers and trainers may display, especially when working one-to-one. Having a structured, step-by-step learning process makes it easier for the champion to work positively and patiently in manageable stages with the individual learner. Consolidating at the end of each of these stages helps to ensure that the learning progresses positively. Getting this flowing smoothly will help the champion to maintain his patience!

Focus Time 5.1

Under the section "Learning progressions" in Chapter 4 (Page 46), we saw the progression of Knowledge / Comprehension / Application illustrated for both factual and practical areas. Slightly later, in our motoring example, the progressive stages were illustrated, showing the learning develop in "chunks" of applied information.

This is one of the key foundations of our approach to learning – building learning graduall on progressive, solid levels and letting each settle through manageable consolidation.

Bearing in mind the three-step formula, look at the following example. Parallel with each stage, try to think of an information area where you might act as a champion for an individual learner – make notes separately of the stages of progress you might follow.

Example: Writing meeting minutes

Stage 1.
Knowledge: List terminology used
Comprehension: Review definitions
Application: Discuss terminology in minutes example
Stage 2.
K: Review structure of minutes layout
C: Discuss reasons for including expected detail
A: Write sample summaries at this detail level
Stage 3.
K: Identify key information discussed in meeting
C: Review against detail required in minutes

A: Write appropriate summary statements

Stage 4.

K: Establish preferred structure and writing style / content

C: Draft this out for meeting (from information in Stage 3)

A: Write draft structured minutes, for review

This four-stage process will give an easy-to-follow progression which allows the empowered learner to build the ideas logically. It will also enable him/her to check very easily that any subsequent practical exercises and examples are including all the necessary steps and stages. This is the very important element of consolidating the learning positively.

Spend a little time planning and noting your own model in parallel with this example, concentrating on presenting the information in progressive (Knowledge/Comprehension/ Application) sections.

We will return to the importance of regular consolidations slightly later in this chapter – but bear in mind that it's an integral part of the Application in the "bite-sized chunks" approach. The individual learner must demonstrate understanding of the detail of section one before moving on to section two ... and so on. The champion must remember to check this level of understanding at each stage.

If there's anything that the learner doesn't properly understand at any given level, the next levels of information are likely to suffer from being built on those shaky foundations below. Visualise this as a building under construction. The higher levels of our property will become unstable where the lower levels of brickwork are poorly constructed or finished. Thinking in terms of our "bite-sized chunks", the learner is trying to eat the next chunk before s/he's properly digested the present one. Result – competency indigestion! This is of course true for all types of learning. Progressive consolidation is key to effective information retention.

Champions will understand the needs of others better if they can remind themselves periodically of some learning area where they personally can easily find themselves outside their "learning comfort-zone". Memories of these personal blockages will help us relate to any special needs of our individual learners. This will help to maintain patience and understanding – and will encourage us to think of alternative ways of re-explaining the detail, to overcome the blockage and progress positively once again.

Focus Time 5.2 – Some simple techniques

There's no intention here, remember, of training a workplace champion to become a professional trainer or presenter. The key issue is that s/he can transfer the information in a clear way, check understanding – and respond to any confusion by potentially explaining things in a variety of different ways.

The additional role which is easier for the on-site champion to achieve than a classroom trainer is the oversight of the new information being applied and reinforced in the workplace. This, including any small injections of remedial suggestions to overcome blockages and maintain progress, is one of the key assets of our workplace championing model.

Just think of the overall benefits, in co-operative teamwork and motivated atmosphere as well as through the development of individual competencies. It is, as they say, awesome!

In order that the workplace champion can do this, the development programme should concentrate on practising the following techniques:

- *explaining detail using straight forward (jargon-free) language;*
- *thinking in the "bite-sized chunks" discussed previously;*
- *using open questioning (how, why, what, when, where, who?);*
- *applying listening skills to identify specific problems;*
- *setting up practical exercises which directly reinforce the theory; and*
- *developing ways of establishing and monitoring standards.*

These are largely issues of effective communication – encouraging the champion to get the message across clearly, at the correct level for each individual learner. Notice that statement – different learners understand and respond at different levels. As with other forms of teaching, this is one of the real potential benefits of the one-to-one techniques we're advocating, when the champion takes the time to establish and respond to each individual learner's current level of knowledge and skill.

The final two bullet points are both involved with monitoring the new skills and techniques which the individual has learned – and on checking that the achievement levels are maintained through day-on-day use in the workplace.

Focus Time 5.3

Think of the key learning required in simple food handling.

Stripping aside much of the detail of different pathogens, clothing and temperature control equipment, we can establish the key areas of:

- *personal hygiene and food handling*
- *fundamentals of temperature control*

Get these right, and most of the problems will be under control.

Referring to the bullet points at the start of this section, you'll see that elements like simple language, presented in digestible chunks and an active dialogue between the champion and individual learner are important.

So, some of the important information which needs to be covered would be:

- *the importance of personal hygiene and hand washing;*
- *the fact that protective clothing exists to protect the food, not the operative;*
- *the key issues relating to food handling and clean surfaces / equipment;*
- *the separate storing of raw and cooked food – with reasons; and*
- *temperature control – related to keeping food chilled, and cooking thoroughly.*

Much of this can be learned through discussion and demonstration. Most of it is straight forward. Knowing WHY things are important will reinforce the need to carry them out consistently. Because the champion will be around when the individual learner is putting his/her new learning into practice, the all-important reinforcement and maintenance of standards will be relatively easy to provide.

From your own experiences of eating in restaurants or shopping in supermarkets, you'll be aware of some of the areas where standards can slip, such as:

- *a chef having a smoke outside by the bins in full kitchen uniform;*
- *handling cold meat pies and raw steak without washing hands between;*
- *meat slicers being used for different cold meats without being cleaned;*
- *a cook having a general hand-wipe cloth, which is used for all purposes;*
- *protective latex gloves being worn during a range of different activities;*
- *cooked food left out on an open surface for some time, prior to use; or*
- *raw meat (especially poultry) not being cooked long or hot enough.*

Think for a few moments about how you could:

1. *Explain some of these key standards to a new food handler.*
2. *Set up a way of monitoring day-to-day practice to maintain standards.*

Using practical reinforcement to consolidate learning

We need to consider other means of consolidating the learning through reinforcement. In designing formal classroom training, this can sometimes be a problem, either because it can be hard to set up a realistic practical situation or because the trainer is attempting to use some pre-designed, general exercise which is not necessarily totally relevant.

Workplace championing is directed at preparing someone to be able to achieve a particular activity in the workplace – or to improve their competency in that activity. Because the development is taking place in the workplace, it should be easier to link the practical exercises directly with the particular activities practised there. Both the champion and the empowered learner will be aware of it, as the activity will be one which occurs naturally (and probably regularly) within the department.

So, for example, if the individual learner needs to learn a unique new process which is applied in the department, learning it in situ will be more relevant than attending a company wide training event. There, various slightly different processes might be reviewed to satisfy the cross-departmental needs of delegates, potentially causing confusion for any single delegate. One-to-one championing will both focus on the uniqueness of the need and ensure the responsive follow-up consolidation.

The key areas of knowledge for championing activities

Where the learner's development is more about taking in factual information than performing an activity, the exercises will focus on reinforcing the knowledge and understanding of this newly learned information. As long as the champion doesn't lose sight of the specific outcome and the fact that the learner currently lacks competency in actually practising this outcome – it should be pretty clear what the required reinforcement will be. Responding to workplace needs means we're tending to think in reverse – we can see what the required result or outcome is, so the input we then devise is building towards achieving this result.

As well as establishing a clear objective or outcome, there are several criteria involved in the champion setting up an effective practical exercise. These include:

- having all the facilities and materials available for it to happen;
- giving enough (undisturbed) time for the outcome to be achieved;
- providing a detailed-enough initial briefing to remove doubts and fears; and
- including the availability of on-going support to maintain progress.

Ensuring that this preparation takes place prior to starting the learning activity will allow things to proceed more smoothly, giving a better guarantee of success.

Establishing and overcoming blocks to progress

Here, we have a further extension to setting up and monitoring practical reinforcement and progress. Theories relating to forward planning underline that the experienced champion will be in a strong position to identify potential blocks to progress, if he is aware of:

the expected outcome

↓

practical workplace conditions and constraints

↓

the particular competencies and skills-level of the learner

We also believe that, through empowerment, the learner can progressively develop this level of awareness, if encouraged to be openly conscious of his/her strengths and shortfalls. It is a truism but still worth repeating that, if the possible reasons for blocks can be identified before the obstruction actually happens, there is a greater likelihood of taking action to avoid impediments. The end result will be that there are fewer problems because a greater percentage of problems are anticipated and bypassed.

In relation to our 7 "C"s:

- **competent**
- consistent
- **conversant**
- credible
- **creative**
- communicative
- co-operative

we're focused on the **creative** reaction to **conversant competence**.

Focus Time 5.4

Consider the principle of defensive driving – which is based on the driver focusing further ahead than s/he would normally look, in order to identify and respond to potential hazards.

For example, you, as the driver, may see a vehicle in the distance, drawing out from a side road to cross your path. Reducing your acceleration will allow it to cross over to the other lane before you arrive at the junction. Your journey has only been delayed by seconds, your stress level is the same as before and the possibility of screeching tyres and buckled metalwork has been reduced dramatically.

We believe that many of the problems created within business are caused by poor communication – either through lack of – or inappropriate – or incomplete detail. Much of this could also be reduced or even eliminated if some forward thought and planning had been applied.

You can't always pre-judge what a potential block will be – we don't live in a perfect world – so life is perhaps not quite as simple as indicated above. We believe that it is valuable to think through possible alternative options to particular situations, from time to time. As well as exercising the mind, it means that you have devised a range of strategies, which makes it easier to respond when a specific crisis ultimately arrives. This is the principle of forward strategy planning – considering and comparing different options before you need them, so that they're more manageable when you finally do.

Action Time 5.1

One particular problem which often occurs when setting up a championing event is ***guaranteeing an uninterrupted period of time to carry out the workplace championing and achieve our agreed outcome.*** *If it doesn't happen, the flow of learning will be interrupted and the outcome will be less than expected.*

We've doubtless all experienced the excuses given. From facilities not being available, to a noisy office, to the Manager not wishing to release the learner.

In the first case, the workplace championing session should be postponed – and rescheduled for a time as soon as possible when both parties can concentrate properly.

In the other cases, a little preparation, communication and planning would mainly resolve the issues before they became a problem. It does raise one important issue, however. It underlines the fact that the champion needs to have some degree of influence in the department and business. Where this is less likely due to reasons of job status, champions must be able to expect consistent support from more senior management. Consistent support as the championing model evolves is paramount.

The types and implications of different learning styles

We've already considered learning styles briefly and established that there is a very wide variety on offer. One such is the Honey and Mumford Learning Styles Inventory – the full instruments are available through Peter Honey's website (http://www.peterhoney.com). Like many other questionnaire-driven systems, this gives you a method of scoring your preferred styles under a range of different titles: in the case of this instrument –

- Activist
- Theorist

- Pragmatist
- Reflector

Before we go into some of the characteristics of the different styles, it's fair to underline that virtually nobody has a total bias towards a single style. Individual preferences are represented on the instrument as points on a pair of crossed axes. When the four points are joined to form some permutation of a skewed quadrilateral, the shape will indicate each individual's relative degree of preferred styles visually. People usually finish up with some permutation of this distorted diamond, with the bias towards two or three of the faces.

It's also important to note that an individual may prefer different styles for particular areas of learning ... a formal talk and discussion to learn new theory, while still preferring a highly active, open-ended hands-on approach, to put that theory into practice. So, the benefit to the workplace champion of carrying out such exercises is to underline the importance of variety in learning. They also act as a guide for –

- selecting appropriate styles of learning for particular subject areas;
- matching learning activities with the individual learner's preferences;
- relating to each learner's starting point of knowledge and skill; and
- responding pro-actively to particular learning needs and potential blockages.

Key Characteristics of different learning styles

Activists

- leap enthusiastically into new experiences;
- will tend to learn by trial and error;
- are open-minded and unquestioning;
- enjoy crisis fire fighting and being the centre of attention; and
- get bored easily – interested in immediate rather than longer term.

Theorists

- have analytical minds and enjoy applying theories;
- think through problems in a logical, step-by-step way;
- are perfectionists who like everything to fit into systems;
- do not respond well to subjective or lateral thinking; and
- can be slightly pedantic, while evolving their detailed theories.

Pragmatists

- enjoy applying new theories in practice;
- take every opportunity to experiment with and adapt new ideas;
- get frustrated with people who prefer to talk rather than act;
- are very practical and enjoy hands-on problem solving; and
- are recognised as "out of the box" thinkers.

Reflectors

- tend to consider things from a range of different view points;
- need to evaluate evidence carefully before choosing to act;
- can be more interested in the planning than the implementation;
- enjoy watching others in action – and learning about their skills; and
- can have a remote, tolerant attitude – but do respond to others' ideas.

Reading through these various characteristics will give you some ideas why **you** prefer to learn certain things in certain ways. Just remember that the same variety works for your championing sessions with different individual learners. Be flexible!

Awareness of the different styles suggests why activists and theorists have problems working together – and why even pragmatists get frustrated at the ways of theorists, which they may perceive as rather ponderous and unimaginative. Put this in the context of the potentially different preferred styles represented by each pair of workplace champion and learner and you'll see why maintaining an awareness of learning styles helps to make interactions more positive.

Satisfying the range of learning styles

So, the range of preferred styles represented by the group of delegates on a formal training course can become a potential problem for the trainer to satisfy, especially as the structure normally preferred in a formalised training course may bias the session towards the use of more theoretical or reflective techniques. Some of the ideas incorporated in accelerated learning are applied most effectively when coaching activists – but may not be best for delivering sequential information.

The more you study the characteristics and apply them in a range of learning situations, the more you'll discover why some learning events are more successful than others ... and why some individuals learn better than others in any given situation. It's a fascinating subject – and one which any budding workplace champion should spend some time considering and applying.

Monitoring the achievement of competencies

If we're saying that a champion is someone who has been identified as being:

a) competent and experienced in the particular activity to be studied; and
b) able to transfer this knowledge and skill to others (with help as required)

– it follows that the workplace champion should be aware of the final levels of competency expected from the learner.

S/he is unlikely, however, to be fully aware of how to analyse and specify this. An in-depth analysis will include:

- the detail to be included;
- standards to be achieved;

- sub-divisions of activities;
- logical progression of these activities; and
- measurements of success

– involved in achieving the particular competency level.

Someone directly involved in training might be expected to be able to dissect any competency into its component elements, before building these back up into a training programme (although even some less-experienced training officers may have difficulty doing this in sufficient detail).

Our expectations of the workplace champion, defined as being a competent practitioner in his particular skills areas but with only part-time involvement in training and developing others, will be more general. As s/he is intimately aware of the skills and knowledge involved in the subject area being championed, we might expect a strong awareness of the ultimate competency standards involved.

However, it's probable that s/he would still need assistance in covering the range of analysis skills bulleted above, in order to work stage by stage with the empowered learner towards achieving expected outcome competency levels. These are some of the more formal areas of development for our prospective workplace champions.

Linking championing with traditional coaching

Action Time 5.2 – Activity Case Study

Imagine I'm playing tennis and you're my coach.
Too many of my cross-court returns are hitting the top of the net – it's as obvious to me as it is to you that my returns are lacking height ... and power. But what do we do about it? Let's say that you, as coach, discuss possibilities with me until we agree that it's the power and twist of my wrist action that requires attention. I (the individual learner) will be as involved as you (the coach) in analysing my actions and suggesting remedial fine tuning. This might include a general wrist strengthening requirement, addressed off the tennis court and in the gym. As well as the overall power, however, we may agree that there is a need to focus on getting more of a lift into the return, by concentrating on the wrist action when the racquet makes contact with the ball.

In-depth focus

So, we've narrowed down the whole arena of me moving around the court and making my low cross-court returns – to a focus on my wrist action. Having addressed the strengthening of my wrist muscles by other means, we can really concentrate on this wrist action when making a closely monitored sequence of returns.

It should be clear what's happening from the championing point of view when considering a visual, physical action like this – but the elements of coaching are applied equally in cognitive (or knowledge) activities as well.

Action Time 5.3 – Information Case Study

Taking another scenario, perhaps our next particular individual learner has a key problem with some element of English grammar and syntax (the difference between "its" and "it's", for example). So, as well as giving him/her direct factual input about the rules which apply, we could look at examples of his/her writing, isolate uses of "its"/"it's" and analyse which were correct usage and which were errors.

Once again, there is a progression of steps and stages, with each one building on the previous input(s). How would the on-going consolidation work here? Most importantly, the champion would offer an "open door" policy for the next few times that the individual learner requires to write the "its/it's" word, to allow for a quick check, either to confirm correctness or explain remedially.

That added action should cement the correct usage (with, for the record, "its" being a possessive pronoun used like "his" and "it's" being an abbreviation of "it is"). If there is still any doubt about confident use, the champion could briefly check through the individual learner's written work periodically, to pick up on any remaining confusion.

Interpersonal Skills – simulated exercises

If the individual learner has a problem with interpersonal skills, the champion might observe him/her in action, identify where mistakes were made and then the two would spend reflective time considering alternative strategies. This method is often used in monitoring call centre assistants' competencies. This use of real workplace interactions could cause problems, as the individual learner is in effect practising by "trial and error" on the public, using live calls. There is a real safety and benefit in using simulated exercises in the initial stages, with the supervisor or colleague acting as the "customer".

As with our tennis case study, a similar focus on particular tips and techniques can happen in these simulations, with later applications in real workplace situations then positively reinforcing and refining the learning. This reduces the likelihood of any problems arising through trying things out fresh on customers.

Action Time 5.4 – Illustrative Case Study

A few years ago, my company produced a complete open learning programme for Customer Service Assistant training for one of the international courier companies.

In our analysis discussions, we established that preferred practice would be to set up simulated exercises using an off-line system and supervisors or buddies acting as the customer. The reality of the situation was, however, that this self-study package would be used throughout twelve European countries, with many of the offices quite small and lacking the facilities for off-line work. A compromise had to be reached.

We responded by producing a range of simulated exercises which the individual could practise using the live system, with strong emphasis on the fact that activities must stop at a point before the data was downloaded into the system. We also set up ring-fenced training files in the live system, which could be used for complete processes without entering ghost packages into the system – which would have caused problems for the real receiving locations identified in the theoretical exercises.

The exercises worked well – although best practice, in an ideal situation, would still favour simulation off-line. The point here is that the needs and applications were both different and specific, so the response was best-suited to meet these needs.

Keep an open mind and don't stick unnecessarily to prescribed ways of doing things, when adaptations will work better.

Focus Time 5.5

Using the above as models, think through one or two examples of situations where structured learning has taken place – perhaps direct experiences you have had yourself or which you have seen in operation in your workplace.

Try to identify:

- *particular learning issue(s) or objectives which were identified;*
- *areas where facts and knowledge were imparted (traditional mentoring);*
- *remedial attention to refining particular elements (traditional coaching);*
- *activities (such as tutoring, questioning etc) used to reinforce learning; and*
- *the perceived strengths and shortfalls of the overall championing.*

Monitoring standards

Because we've established that the workplace champion must be proficient in any skill s/he will be involved in delivering to others, we can agree fairly confidently that s/he should be aware of expected overall competencies and outcomes. We've already agreed that s/he may require some assistance in breaking this up into a sequence of steps and stages, in order that the empowered learner can work progressively towards achieving this competency. This is like climbing a set of stairs, where the champion must identify the goal or outcome at each step – it's the bite-sized chunks approach again!

As an extension to this, some champions might lack direct experience of monitoring achievement of learning standards in an on-going, progressive way – and responding pro-actively to any deterioration spotted. If s/he is also a supervisor or manager, monitoring and maintaining standards should be part of his/her day-to-day activities. Applying it in a learning and development context can, however, still create unique difficulties and does require additional consideration.

Maintaining learning standards

It's natural for people's performance – or competency achievement – to level off in phases, as speed increases. Think about when you learned some particular new skill – let's take a simple example of producing a particular item.

Initially, you might concentrate on being able to produce a single example – slowly but correctly.

Then, as you gained in confidence, you gradually speeded up – so that after a while, you were not only able to produce the item to quality standards but could also keep going and gradually produce several. In doing this, you were moving towards achieving the quantity standard as well. However, at this point, it is quite normal for quality standards to slip as the learner concentrates more on producing quantities.

If you experience this quality deterioration when involved in championing, it's possible to reduce the quantity target, to allow the individual learner to concentrate on the issues of inferior quality. Then, when the quality standard has been achieved once more, the focus can then return to racking up the quantity once more.

This is likely to recur periodically, giving a sequence of peaks and troughs as the individual learner gradually progresses towards confident competency.

The on-going picture

This situation continues with the proficient employee as well, of course – in order to maintain required standards. It's to be expected that our performance may plateau out periodically, through familiarity, boredom, frustration or restricted challenges. It's important that the root cause is identified ... the potential knee-jerk reaction of "re-training" in response to sub-standard work is often not the real answer to the problem.

The champion as monitor

It's an awareness of these kinds of activities and responses that allow any workplace champion to monitor the learner's progress towards both achieving and maintaining competency levels. Think of it as a sliding scale – you could visualise it more as a chute than a set of stairs – so it can be difficult sometimes to be specific about intermediate reference points. The development milestones, with their requirement for reinforcement and practice, may also vary between individual learners.

The integrated triangle model

In our wide-ranging model, where the champion could potentially be lower in the business hierarchy than the learner for specific subject areas, we could have a further complication. The atmosphere has to be right for any "criticism" to be seen in the more positive light of being "development assistance"! Our goal is for workplace championing to be incorporated into the overall business activity. Where this is gradually achieved, and it is accepted that people of all ranks shall be helping each other, a co-operative atmosphere should become a natural progression, resulting in a more level hierarchy.

When in place, objective discussion and concept-sharing should be more possible across the spectrum of the organisation. Of course, degrees of objectivity across a complete workforce will always vary, so we may probably never achieve complete harmony. Strive for the critical mass point, which can tip the balance towards making co-operation the norm rather than the exception.

Maintaining a positive, motivating work atmosphere

This is a key foundation which underpins all attempts at introducing positive development into a business. It's very evident, when you think about it. It's been a recurring underlying theme throughout this book, when we've been considering areas such as "bigger picture thinking"; "long-term management support"; "non-shifting goalposts" and the concept of individuals openly helping each other.

Consider the seven "C"s of holistic workplace success once more –

- *competency*
- *consistency*
- *conversance*

- ***credibility***
- ***creativity***
- ***communication***
- ***co-operation***

Of these, consistency is probably the most crucial, when trying to introduce and promote the wide-ranging concept of workplace championing within an organisation. This consistency is crucial to maintaining positive progress. As already stated, it's better to initially reduce the scope – and even to pick only those that are the most positive-thinking individuals and departments – in order to be surer of this progress. Having been selective to give yourself – and the process – the greatest chance of success, you can then focus on gradually encouraging everyone involved to think in a more altruistic, holistic way.

Consistency

Consistency doesn't, of course, mean getting stuck in the same old rut. This is where creativity enters the equation. This implies change as fine adjustment in the light of experience rather than constant change for the sake of it. Some of this may appear unrealistic – even idealistic – but careful consideration might indicate that the constant change option is creating a stressful, demotivating culture which does little for co-operative working.

Universal holistic attitudes can encourage today's individualistic thinkers to understand the benefits of giving as well as receiving.

Some of the key tenets for a more holistic life, which are relevant to developing a consistently positive work atmosphere, are:

- build positive thought;
- be aware of yourself and others;
- believe in yourself and others;
- act as selflessly as you can;
- allow time to do things properly;
- give matters time to evolve;
- work towards co-operation and away from egocentricity;
- consider the effects of your actions;
- do what ultimately feels right; and
- amend your plans openly to maintain progress.

The greater the number of people who can be encouraged to embrace these ideals, the more likely that positive work and life co-operation will evolve and become established. Think of them as the milestones on the holistic route to workplace development.

Company processes and key business objectives

Company processes and key business objectives form part of appraisals, board meetings, training needs analysis and management objectives. We should therefore expect that directors, managers and those involved in training and development should be aware of them – and understand their relevance in directing and developing business. It is, however, perhaps fair to judge that some managers, although aware of the business objectives which affect their department directly, may not be too clued up(!) as to the implications of overall company objectives across the breadth of the company.

So, when we consider specific workplace champions, who could be at any level within the organisation, we cannot assume too broad an awareness of company processes and key business objectives. They might be aware of those that affect them on a daily basis but these could be quite restricted. We should be in a position to expect them to know their specialist processes and objectives in detail. The broader awareness can be gradually introduced and supported.

Standardisation of key processes

It saves a lot of time, effort – and potentially problems – if key processes are standardised. The company in which I am currently employed has worked on consultancy projects with several national corporations to re-establish and implement agreed processes. These exercises had become necessary because changes of personnel over a period of time had created confusion by promoting slightly different "takes" on individual processes. It's the "sitting with Nellie" problem again, where different views and applications evolve over the years and compete for acceptance.

Once the processes have been agreed and standardised once more, it provides an official reference point (or standard operational procedure) for all involved to follow. This is what lies behind bench marking, quality assurance and other forms of standards setting. The final process is often quite simple, once the complications and confusions have been stripped away. There's nothing wrong with simplicity!

Benefits and applications of standardisation

As well as creating a norm, of course, standardisation also makes imitation easier for our competitors. Think once more of our concept of Creative Consistency – we may aspire to meet the benchmark consistently. Companies benchmark against each other – most supermarkets probably strive towards achieving Tesco's benchmarks. Meanwhile, Tesco is doubtless reviewing and enhancing its own benchmarks progressively. Setting, refining and improving upon your company benchmarks will usually encourage beneficial responses. Constant, pressure-blinded raising of targets which lack both consistency and creativity is demotivating – and is one of the key causes of the work-related stress which is pervading business.

We will come later to some basic learning delivery design and planning techniques which our workplace champions should be assisted in applying. If we're spreading our champion net as wide as possible, we cannot assume that they possess anything like this level of awareness. For example, a technically-written process guide is often too complex to be used directly as a learning resource. It may appear clear to the proficient user but, in his role as champion, it will undoubtedly need some "translation" before being useful to the new individual learner. This is where checklists and other learning resources are valuable. The Development Support Function of our integrated model should take the initiative in helping to source these to meet the workplace champion's specific needs.

Key inter-relationships within and between departments

Workplace champions should be aware of the relationships which exist within and between departments. Sometimes, these will operate because of office politics. At other times, it'll be a case of allowing the champion to identify additional reference sources for information, process detail or specific experience.

As our techniques encourage workplace championing to extend within the organisation, it's likely that champion/learner interactions may gradually expand to work between separate departments, where specialist inputs are required. Where a co-operative, holistic atmosphere has been generated, particular experts can be encouraged to offer support to individual learners throughout the organisation, rather than merely within their own department. Again, this evidently requires monitoring and organisation – the system can be rapidly debased where some champions begin to feel either (or both) over-taxed or taken for granted. If managed properly, however, using "star champions" like this is a way of propagating high standards and consistency.

Inter-departmental co-operation – and competition

Cross-departmental championing is also very valuable where the work of different departments inter-relates – as it so often does. However, it can be quite difficult getting departments to work closely together, especially where an atmosphere of inter-departmental competition and rivalry is current corporate policy, or if some departments do not see the value of others. Historically, for example, exclusive Administration and Personnel/Human Resources departments were created to support the activities of the mainstream productive Business – releasing them from having to spend time on certain documentation, for example. Staff in the Business departments may not feel that those in Admin and HR have jobs of equivalent worth, and/or that the requests for information they send through (such as to fill out sample applications) serve only to inhibit their own production.

Thinking positively, however, individuals assisting each other as champions within and between departments will create an atmosphere where general company co-operation is more likely to develop. This will evolve from informal networking as much as, if not more than, from any organised arrangements. This will exist as long as a positive co-operative atmosphere, without hidden agendas, can be maintained.

Growing our champions

There is a wide range of techniques that workplace champions can learn and apply, in order to develop that co-operative working atmosphere. Many are to do with gaining a better understanding of structure and sequence; some are to do with the skills of working positively one-to-one with others. Through initial selection, some of the skills may be innate – and already existing in some of the champions. As we progressively involve more and more champions in the process, their training and development will require a mix of "bite-sized" training and on-going reinforcement. Using these one-to-one development techniques to gradually improve individual skills-shortfall areas is giving the champion first hand experience of being an individual learner – thereby helping them to see things from both sides.

6 Setting up the Championing System

One-minute overview

In this chapter, we're focusing on setting up the championing system, within the integrated approach. We review the importance of flexibility – and the key requirements for planning for and monitoring progress. The importance of receiving support and maintaining the momentum are seen as paramount – and the conditions and skills necessary for these to succeed are discussed. The chapter examines how we identify both individual learners and workplace champions – and lists some of the development areas necessary for champions, to allow them to work in a constructive way. The final sections look at selling the benefits, keeping the momentum going and the first considerations regarding the support and administration of the expanding programme.

The integrated approach to workplace championing

Within our model, the integrated cyclical approach we have been advocating is referred to as 360 degree championing. This two and multi-way transfer of knowledge and skills throughout an organisation is a flexible and specific way of reacting rapidly to individual development needs. As a technique it:

- responds to specific shortfall areas;
- encourages staff co-operation;
- involves support in providing realistic responses;
- presents good value for money;
- reduces training course expenditure; and
- targets money where it can be of greatest internal value.

Setting up the new system

When trying to implement any major change, it's crucial that the first attempts are positive – and are seen by others to be both positive and successful. Achieving this requires a whole range of criteria, which, once established, must be maintained. If the outcomes subsequently require amendment, the overall objective must be revisited rapidly and openly, to make sure that any changed priorities are accommodated positively. This will allow a revised set of outcomes to be quickly re-established and work to progress once more.

This is true for any major change process in business. It's equally true for setting up and progressing with our workplace championing model.

Championing the champions

Workplace championing must be seen to be a positive use of time for everyone directly involved. So, although high-level training skills are not the order of the day, a planned structure, which keeps everyone moving forward in the process, is crucial.

Facilitation skills – **knowing how to make smooth progress** – on the part of any overall co-ordinator will help ensure that everyone continues to be motivated – and that the decisions made will match their particular styles and preferences.

Remember that this whole process is based on one-to-one activities, so each activity can focus on the needs of the specific champion and individual learner involved. We're definitely not going down the "one size fits all" route here.

Focus Time 6.1

Many of us will have been in a situation of working on a new project which went wrong – either because the criteria or ground rules changed, staffing altered during the project life, the necessary technology was not available ... or one of the many other reasons why project plans can go adrift.

However impressive the project planning looks on paper, one of the problems for Training is that its involvement in the design and development of responses usually appears near the end of the chain. Not only can this impact on the time available for effective training but as it is the case that it is often only close to the final dates, when the detail of a project has become clearer, that the stark reality of previous decisions and the associated operational implications are actually realised, there is the likelihood of disruption to any training response that has been designed.

Learning lessons – flexible timing

One of the key lessons as far as informal championing is concerned is that the timing of training timescales must be as flexible as possible. Development times are being scheduled within normal workloads for the champion as well as the individual learner – so we must maintain a voluntary atmosphere around the agreement.

Where the need for coaching, mentoring or other inputs has reached emergency proportions (as with an operational crisis or new priority skill requirement), the needs level will of course escalate, and the championing input will be arranged and executed as immediately as possible.

Look for the WIN–WIN outcome

If you study negotiation skills, the preferred outcome is the WIN–WIN result – where both (or all) parties feel that they have gained something. This is what we're aiming to achieve when promoting workplace championing involvement.

Key requirements for a successful development

When planning those first championing activities, we want to:

- start small and controllable;
- identify a supportive atmosphere (department, team or even group);
- nurture the support, compromising if necessary;
- identify a development need which will give noticeable results;
- ensure that this need is important to the business;
- select the first batch of learners who are likely to be responsive; and
- identify and develop your first champion(s) with extra care.

When our first workplace champion programme is up and running we must:

- set up a timetable and monitor its progress;
- ensure that the development support is in place and working;
- arrange for individual champions to receive any additional support;
- guarantee that the workplace reinforcement is happening;
- help the champion(s) organise any remedial input to receivers;
- ensure the receiver gets opportunities to apply these new skills; and
- start identifying the next areas requiring high-value championing.

Let's consider some of these as a gradual progression –

1. Preparing the foundations
2. Identifying the key players
3. Initial activities
4. Keeping things progressing positively

1. Preparing the foundations for the new development

First find a positive thinking environment, which is (or can be encouraged to be) receptive to the whole idea of workplace championing. You should be looking to identify a functional department which is enthusiastic towards training and development generally. Perhaps that department's management has also shown signs of supporting post-course reinforcement of learning in the past. This might indicate that they can envisage the benefits of on-site workplace learning and embrace general skills succession planning.

Once the department(s) is/are identified, the next stage is to establish priority departmental learning and development needs. Notice, this identification is coming from within the department – the need(s) must be seen as requiring action and response – with the activity resulting in some added value for the department itself. It's not the time to implement new company initiatives.

Establishing support for the development

Before discussing the practicalities of running a programme in detail, it's essential to establish clearly that senior management within the department (who might include you!) are supportive of the ideas. Perhaps one key issue here is time management. As well as agreeing to the release of individual learners for short periods, managers must also accept that identified champions will require uninterrupted periods to support the development programme. The champions may also, where necessary, need to prepare before some events. This preparation is important – champions (who will in the main not have a background in organised learning) need time to think through how to get the message over clearly.

Keeping the momentum going

Many of us will have experienced the situation where a new initiative starts off dynamically with initial management support and enthusiasm. However, just as we feel it's beginning to show results and has encouraged additional ideas, some manager grows weary of the effort involved and blocks further staff release.

It's certainly true that releasing staff for any form of training and development activities makes management and day-to-day scheduling harder. However, workplace champion programming will usually involve short sessions on-site and will always be more time effective than removing staff totally to attend longer training events. As an added bonus, the on-going workplace reinforcement which is part of the learning process means that the learner is directly – and more effectively – productive again as rapidly as possible.

It's very important at this stage that –

- any management and organisational concerns are talked through and hopefully resolved;
- these discussions are facilitated by someone who's strongly aware of and enthusiastic about the championing system's function and benefits;
- any operational plans are designed to suit the particular environment;
- the more supportive managers within a department are involved; and
- enthusiastic departmental sections or teams are initially identified, to give the best potential degree of success.

In the longer term, it's hoped that these initial, if localised, positive results will prove to others that there are benefits from involvement! When former doubters approach the championing co-ordinators to request involvement in future workplace development projects, we know the process is beginning to evolve successfully.

Working on the assumption for the moment that we've managed to establish a supportive atmosphere within a particular department, we can now begin to focus on the particular needs and shortfalls. Again, to illustrate benefits, we should be looking for a development area which will give major impact to the business. This could, for example, be where there's currently a shortage of competent staff. Alternatively, it might be in response to a situation where standards are slipping because of a general competency problem, experienced by several staff members.

This stress on achieving positive impact throughout the company may appear slightly manipulative. However, the public celebration of success at sorting out some major skills shortage will provide valuable internal publicity. New initiatives such as workplace championing need this type of publicity to become recognised. The importance of achieving success from the outset should be self evident.

Spotlighting our first individual learners

Establishing a particular need area will automatically highlight the staff members requiring assistance – the two go hand in hand. We need to get them actively involved – these are potentially our first batch of individual learners.

To achieve a closer guarantee of success, we're seeking to pinpoint a development area where some combination of one-to-one coaching and mentoring is the best technique. In order to make our early attempts manageable, we'd also be wise to look for a key area with relatively small numbers of individuals needing development.

The details of each individual's shortfalls are likely to vary between different learners. Champions should be encouraged to respond flexibly to meeting individual learning priorities. This is one of the key benefits of the system. However, some champions may need assistance to achieve competency in this – analysing and responding specifically is considered a fairly high-level skill, even for professional trainers or teachers.

Our pilot group

So, at this stage in the process, we should have established our first small group of individual learners, all requiring development in a similar learning area. Although considering the same shortfall, each may potentially have unique aspects which require specific assistance.

By considering needs widely, we may also have established several additional but distinct remedial areas (with associated individual learners for each) – so we're beginning to see the preferred way forward for the programme.

However, to ensure the success of our first championing activity more confidently, we should initially focus on a single key remedial area. Remember – select for success!

Having established our target department(s), our individual learners and our subject areas, the most obvious outstanding requirement is to identify the initial workplace champions. These are the key players, who will be considered in greater detail in the following section. You, I hope, will want to be one of them!

Additional conditions required

- We need to be sure that all necessary equipment, support materials and technology are available. Because the development will be taking place in or near the learner's normal workplace, it's likely that this should be the case.
- Remember, we can't always use standard on-line equipment for direct training. An operational production belt, for example, might be travelling too fast for a learner to keep up with the operation. A trainee customer services agent involved in logging training-mode data into a live system could create all manner of confusion.
- The operations have to be thought through in order to establish the best way of reinforcing the learning theory. This can involve restricting the input or activity, in a special, training mode; alternatively, it may prove best to set up a simple off-line training environment, if this is technically possible.
- Our developing champions will need assistance in making these types of design and planning decisions. Many are based on the structured thinking we have been advocating. After the first few assisted attempts, these new champions should gain confidence and begin to experiment constructively.

We've already briefly considered the development support corner of the integrated triangle model. If we're expecting workplace champions to volunteer their services, the company should view the provision of necessary learning support positively. In the integrated triangle model, this is seen as being supplied by some combination of

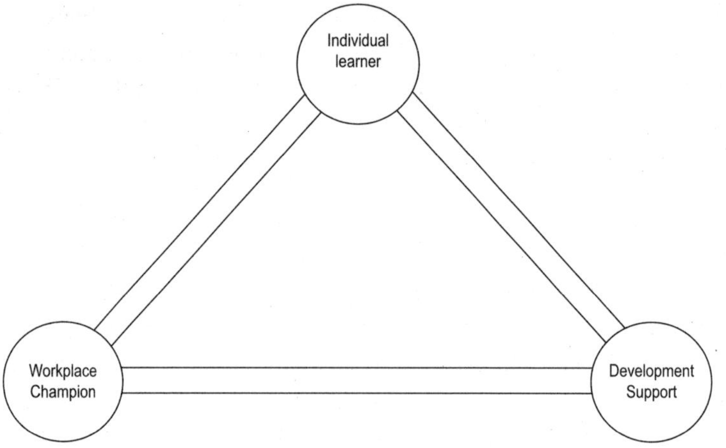

the Training Department, HR, line management and any others who may be able to provide specialist support and materials informally.

Help and support

Champions, once trained, will progressively become capable of planning activities such as dividing their information into manageable "bite-sized chunks". To assist in this self development, they should:

- have access to materials which will help them train;
- be able to call on assistance in arranging their sessions, where required;
- expect support for scheduling time off for their individual learners; and
- benefit from support in arranging their own time off mainstream activities, to devote to workplace development.

This is certainly building a greater expectancy that people will work co-operatively together. We can represent the increasing number becoming involved in the process by imagining the triangle beginning to revolve.

As the roles and responsibilities exchange and merge, we're reaching the point where individuals can be either champion or individual learner at any given moment. At times, s/he will be in the role of individual learner receiving assistance from another champion – while on other occasions, s/he will be acting directly as champion to help someone else. This is the essence of 360 degree championing. This is the beneficial effect of holistic co-operation, bringing a synergy which has a greater end effect than the individual inputs taken together.

2. Identifying the key players – the champions

How do we go about finding our first group of champions?

Having already carried out an initial needs analysis, we'll be clearer about key areas where support through championing is required. Through establishing the need, we'll also be aware of the individual learners requiring assistance.

Initially, it'll be easier to match champions and individual learners within the same department. When identifying potential champions, we'll be looking for people with:

Knowledge and experience of the subject area

Becoming more judgemental about individuals' people skills and soft skills competencies, we'll also be looking for:

- Practical competency (being able to demonstrate the subject effectively).
- Positive attitude towards working with others.
- Good working relationships with senior managers.
- Ability to understand others' learning problems.
- Ability to present information clearly and simply.
- Good communication – able to adjust levels.
- Ordered organisational skills.
- Patience and understanding.
- Ability to manage personal and others' time well.

The question of status and hierarchies in an organisation

Some of these are specific competencies which we would hope to be present in someone with management responsibility over others. However, the model stipulates that it's not necessary for the champion to be in a senior/manager position. Just as attitude is seen as being more important than aptitude, skilful-ness is more important than status.

Junior job status may potentially prove a problem for a workplace champion in certain situations. For example, allocating learning session times or requesting resources or facilities from HR or senior management may prove difficult. Any inter-relationship problems such as these must be addressed and resolved at the early organisational stage. It is vital to gain and maintain support from senior management, to ensure that the workplace championing system works as smoothly as possible.

The growth process for champions

Considering the various criteria above against specific potential champions will highlight the strengths and shortfalls for each. We would then have to balance the rather idealistic achievement of perfection (a champion who is signed off as achieving all listed competency goals) against the need to progress the learning development outcomes as immediately as possible.

We certainly need –

- to have champions who are in a position to succeed;
- high profile examples of individual learners becoming capable of completing an activity to a more competent standard; and
- an appreciable volume of individual learners benefiting from championing.

This brings us to the quality/quantity issue. We need to have a workable number of champions active as soon as possible, so some of these finer skills can be allowed to grow gradually, through experience and remedial assistance.

Expectations and aspirations of champions

We may expect, for example, to be able to identify in champions the previously-noted bullet points:

- understanding of levels
- display of patience
- possession of confidence gained through experience

– and for these to be apparent in the majority of champions initially identified.

We might also accept that basic competency levels relating to elements such as learning design, questioning technique and objective sequencing will probably take longer for some champions to assimilate. However, there will usually be some input necessary, to encourage individual champions to achieve expected basic competency in training others. Techniques might include formalised training or structured open/ e-learning techniques.

Quality and quantity of workplace champions to meet expanding needs

We need to remember that we're ultimately working towards increasing the number of active champions available – and the associated ranges of expertise. There will of course be some specialist workplace champions, involved only in specific skills areas. Others may well assist in a wider range of activities.

Thus, the process must embrace both quality and quantity – to meet the expanding needs as the workplace championing programme begins to take off. With enthusiasm growing as individual learners seek involvement in the workplace championing programme, it's important that the system continues to have enough champions available to respond to the needs within acceptable time-frames.

Necessary support for workplace champions from within the organisation

Support must be expected from:

- the managers directly responsible for the individual learners;
- managers who might have a say in the activities of the champion;
- staff from the training department; and
- others involved in the support and organisation involved in the initiative.

Communication and involvement in the new workplace championing programme

Because there's a change of role and priorities involved, there will be an element of persuasion involved in "selling" the benefits of the new workplace championing ideas to the responsible members of staff bulleted above (such as staff in the training department). It makes sense to keep them informed about progress and to give them warning of any expected involvement in the arrangements. This will also encourage their comment and feedback, allowing them to register observations of how they see the championing programme progressing. They might even offer suggestions as to how they could help with improvements!

3. Initial activities with a learner

Consider the first event. The background preparation is complete and the champion has been briefed – and assisted towards becoming reasonably confident about what s/he has to achieve. What are some of the final checks for the champion, before s/he finally sits down with the designated individual learner and the whole learning development relationship kicks off?

The champion's checklist includes –

- Which particular needs area will I be concentrating on at this session?
- How does it link in with the wider experience of this learner?
- Am I clear as to what the outcome or objective is?
- Will I be able to keep focused and not digress or chat generally?
- Do we both need some time to get to know each other?
- How can I encourage the learner's empowerment from the start?
- Am I clear about the steps and stages we must complete?
- How do I help the learner to become pro-active in the learning?
- What arrangements are needed for reinforcement to happen?
- Have I assembled all the necessary resources and equipment?
- Have I figured out how to consolidate the objective properly?

There's a lot of information there – and some of it infers knowledge of techniques which would need to be covered, as necessary, at the champion's induction.

Assuming this knowledge for the moment, having a clear vision of objective, content and techniques will help the champion get started positively. S/he shouldn't assume, because the session is happening in the workplace, that all the necessary equipment and facilities will be freely available for learning purposes. The reality of having to pause the learning while equipment is located or made ready will disrupt the process and detract from the outcome. It also creates an unprofessional atmosphere, wastes time and can rapidly demotivate the individual learner.

Good champions make time to plan the way forward

Building an initial rapport between champion and learner

It's also important to spend some time building rapport. You may have attended a formal training course as a delegate, where time is spent getting a brief resumé of each delegate's background and reasons for being on the course. You might have felt that this was a device dreamed up by trainers to use up time.

Actually, time spent on getting to know one another can be very useful, if used constructively. Apart from helping to create a more comfortable atmosphere between people, it gives the champion insights into particular problems, related awareness, key individual priorities and the extent of professional and business experience. A good champion can then subsequently use this information positively, to involve delegates and relate the learning to their discussed experiences. In a less formal context, workplace champions can use similar techniques to relate the learning to both the workplace and the learner.

Developing the workplace champion–learner bond

It's likely that the champion and learner already know each other, as they probably work in the same department. Both will be aware of their business environment and priorities – and may already be informed about some of the reasons behind identified problems. The relationship may need to be extended from the initial "colleague workers" level to that of a learning partnership. The initial chat is thus very important, to establish the ground rules and breadth of study required.

Remember – the individual learner's main involvement in professional development to date might have been as a fairly passive learner in a group, waiting for the teacher, trainer or lecturer to tell him/her what to do. There may have been little encouragement for individuals to "think outside the box" creatively.

The champion may have to explain to the individual learner what is involved in being empowered – such as attempting to practise things, or maybe identifying personal blocks, without first being prompted. For some learners, this might even involve a re-education process, if previous formal learning experience has censured them for "stepping out of line". Such encouragement and discussion is part of the mutual development atmosphere which must be introduced during these early stages.

4. Keeping the relationship progressing positively

Having got the process underway, it's important to keep the momentum going. Achieving this by involving additional learners in the same subject is relatively easy. Do remember, however, that each individual learner may potentially benefit from a slightly different approach.

Organisation becomes more complex when the programme is expanded to meet additional workplace championing requirements, in order to respond to new learning needs. This will require the identification of the additional champions necessary. As existing departmental members, this may be relatively easy. The complexity lies in the documenting and management of this ever-enlarging progress. Having some form of CPD (continuing professional development) personal planning system for each learner, such as an I D Plan, will help record progress and indicate future activities.

Once the system is up and running and the positive benefits are recognised, new workplace championing initiatives will be likely to evolve naturally. These can come through:

- additional departmental managers asking to become involved;
- new development areas being identified as benefiting from the process;
- individuals requesting assistance in specific learning areas;
- some existing, "informal help" arrangements being incorporated;

- individuals offering their services as champions for specific tasks; and
- resources coming to light which can assist new championing initiatives.

It's important that any recording system can capture –

- who is involved in championing;
- what development programmes are active;
- how cross relationships between programmes are working;
- which future shortfall areas have been proposed;
- what business priorities have been identified for action;
- what deadlines (individual or business) have been stated;
- how particular championing interactions are progressing; and
- when related resources and organised support are required.

Involving training/HR in workplace championing

This kind of information-gathering can be done centrally within a particular department, responding to the specific needs of that department – or can be monitored overall by the training/HR function. The information and references will be more precise and specific to each department than with general training needs identification. It's important, therefore, that the record keeping is tailored to meet particular championing needs.

We've been suggesting that, once the momentum (or critical mass) point has been reached, new champions are more likely to come forward to volunteer their services. In the earlier stages, it's still likely that we'll have to go through the process of "recruiting" workplace champions. As the HR/training functions are currently the co-ordinators of overall training needs, they'll usually assume the championing co-ordination role as well (singly or in conjunction with departmental managers).

Focus Time 6.2

Think for a moment about your present functional department – and the staff which you have working in it (including yourself, of course!).

Identify around five of the key development areas in which the majority of staff receive some type of training, in order to reach a competency level.

Which of these development areas could be progressed effectively using workplace championing methods? Think about any initial ideas of methods and practical activities which could be applied.

Could you subdivide these under the headings of – Development and Remedial?

Are there any areas where the direct interactions achieved through championing might achieve better learning outcomes than with the techniques currently used?

Which individuals in the department (including yourself, if relevant) would you consider to be competent and experienced in the areas you've identified? Are there any you would identify as being capable of acting as workplace champions?

Think of a few subjects or skills areas in which you might feel confident enough to be able to pass on your knowledge to others.

We've now established how to identify and prepare our first group of champions.

This can be summarised as –

- identify key areas, where change will give a noticeable impact;
- establish individuals with competency, experience and enthusiasm;
- explain range of activities involved in our championing strategy;
- identify differences between this and more formal training involvement;
- discuss the key skills involved in one-to-one workplace championing;
- develop the inter-personal skills necessary to inter-relate effectively;
- establish how to analyse and sequence development needs;
- give straight-forward training in basic learning transfer skills;
- consider the range of ways open for consolidating learning in stages;
- discuss real opportunities for setting up practical reinforcement;
- review ways of working co-operatively with Development Support;
- consider how to apply objective thinking in structuring sessions; and
- review any relationships between different subject and skills areas.

7 Case Study – Improving Greg's and David's Skills Holistically

One-minute overview

This chapter is a full-length case study. It features Greg and David, whom we met in Chapter Three – when they briefly considered some of the issues relating to chairing the Works Council. This case study is a "dramatisation" of a championing session which is in two parts.
The first section considers some of the skills and techniques involved in chairing and managing meetings, while the second section acts as a "fly on the wall" observation of a team applying holistic techniques to plan and organise a group presentation. It examines the development of both learner and champion.

We start the scene in the office of Harry Williams, the departmental manager who is co-ordinating the workplace championing programme in the company. The phone rings.

Hello – Harry Williams speaking.

Hi Harry – it's David Anderson here, from Production 2 Department. Can I ask you something? You know all those ideas about workplace championing which you've been developing in your department ...?

Ye....s

Well, I was wondering if we could meet up sometime to discuss them a bit. I have this young guy Greg who's having a bit of a problem with running meetings – well, really, specifically the Works Council we've set up. I want to help him but would like to do it properly. Is that the kind of area you might be able to help me with?

Yes – it sounds like it. Sure, I'd be pleased to help. Do you plan to get involved in the coaching and mentoring and so on as a workplace champion yourself?

I'd like to try, if I get some pointers as to how to do it properly – but maybe there are others who could help as well?

We're still building up our team of champions, so we're a bit stretched at the moment in our department – perhaps there are one or two others interested within Production itself? I could certainly help with some of the meeting communications bits. Do you want to meet up some time, to talk it through, David?

And so Greg's workplace championing programme was born.

The initial planning meeting

When David and Harry met, they managed to establish some of Greg's key problems. This information would be used as a basis for David's discussion of the way forward with Greg.

These included providing:

- knowledge about the procedures for running a meeting;
- knowledge of how documentation supports meeting structure;

- awareness of the importance of agreeing outcomes/actions;
- attention to keeping better control of time during meetings; and
- proficiency at presenting detail and figures clearly/professionally.

They also established that Greg's key problem was ***not being able to keep on top of the meetings, as he was not assertive enough with meeting members and was not achieving enough progress, nor agreeing outcomes.***

They agreed that, although this appeared to be the key problem, if Greg's awareness of some of the structures and organisation was improved, this would directly result in him achieving better control of meeting progress and the achievement of end results.

Championing the champion

As this exercise was going to be something of a learning event in the skills of championing for David as well, the two agreed that David would take on the role as Greg's champion, with some support from Harry. Harry would act as David's first line development support – as well as helping David learn how to act as a champion for Greg. Harry would in effect be championing David in championing skills. He would also initially liase with HR and Training to make any additional backup support arrangements necessary.

Action Time 7.1

Imagine you're David. You've had your meeting with Harry, as outlined above. Make some notes separately of the key issues you'll discuss with Greg (based on his identified strengths and shortfalls) and plan out a possible programme of learning areas to be covered.

Some learning areas may be better addressed by attending conventional training courses or other techniques rather than championing. If you think this applies to any of your identified subjects, indicate this.

Background research

By asking around, Harry has established that David chairs a variety of meetings and committees, both at work and in his private life – and is rated as knowing a lot about the structure, organisation and documentation areas of running effective meetings.

So, David's experience will be very valuable when applied to his role as champion. As well as the identified areas, Greg has other skills shortfall areas that would benefit from some additional assistance. These include:

- being more assertive;
- managing his time more effectively;
- dealing with and communicating with people better; and
- presenting information at meetings in a more dynamic way.

Each of these problem areas could be addressed by Greg going on a training course – but perhaps some of his needs here are very specific to chairing meetings, so attendance on a fairly general course (although helpful) might not be the best use of Greg's time.

For example –

- Greg's lack of assertiveness might be more the result of confusion and lack of confidence about applying meeting procedures – which remain something of a mystery to him at the moment.
- Time management in meetings is governed by the agenda and a desire to achieve actions or outcomes, so attending a generalised Time Management course would only be of limited value to that specific objective.

Harry agreed to have a word with the HR/Training department to see if they knew of any short Time Management courses or other learning programmes which were geared towards prioritisation and the achievement of actions and outcomes, which would be valuable if applied to running meetings.

The empowered individual learner

David arranged to meet Greg in the company restaurant over lunch and they talked through some of the options open for his development programme. As well as being enthusiastic about learning more, Greg asked if he could sit in at one or two of the meetings that David chaired, to learn by example. Although David wasn't involved with any Works Councils other than the one that Greg chaired, he suggested that Greg might like to sit in at a Project Planning Meeting and an Action-based Production Meeting, which were run along similar lines.

Action Time 7.2

Think of a meeting that you attend, which you would consider to show "best practice". Perhaps its well organised, with the chairperson keeping good control of progress and the achievement of outcomes. Perhaps complex information comes over clearly thanks to good presentation techniques. There is a wide range of skills which all build together to produce the result of an effective, positive meeting.

With this "best practice" in mind, imagine that you are Greg, with the skills deficiencies that we have identified. Think of a variety of questions that he might want to ask David at a debriefing session after the meeting, to clarify achievement.

These might include questions such as:

1. *How do you make sure that everyone gets a chance to speak?*
2. *How do you decide how much information to note down for the minutes?*

Perhaps you can think of a few more?

Progress along the development track

Three weeks have passed and Greg has now been present at two of David's meetings. The next Works Council meeting is due to happen in a fortnight, and David and Greg agree that it would be valuable to have a one hour meeting to discuss key areas for improvement.

At the meeting, David starts off by asking Greg which particular things stood out from the meetings he had watched, as activities that he would like to concentrate on improving. Greg identified the following:

- using the agenda to control the progress of the meeting;
- getting people to "talk through the Chairman" to control arguments;
- using statements of agreed actions to "sign off" agenda items;
- applying techniques to get the quieter members to discuss views; and
- finding out more about using visuals and presenting professionally.

Focus Time 7.1

Think in turn about each of the five activity objectives listed above.

Consider the benefits of improving each activity – and any techniques you've experienced which Greg and David could use to aid this improvement. (Make some notes separately.)

There might be some improvement areas that could be harder to change.

There could, for example, be:

- *too many items on the agenda for completion within the time;*
- *some junior team members who feel they have little to add; and*
- *some aggressive members who dislike being controlled.*

Try to identify a few more areas for improvement.

Can you think of real departmental members who represent these views and attitudes? How might you respond to their needs?

This is an opportunity to relate the theories of championing to your actual experience.

First priorities for David

David decided that the first priority should be sorting out issues about using the agenda – and giving Greg some pointers about writing minutes. Harry had said that he had an idea that he could arrange to allow Greg to sit in on a team presentation-planning meeting and get some ideas about preparing and using visuals – so they'd leave that area to one side for the moment.

After David phoned Harry to see if the company had any useful resources available, Harry popped into his office. He had a small booklet in his hand.

Hi David!

Here's a handy book on writing meeting minutes – perhaps you can copy one or two pages to give to Greg. He doesn't need to give a blow-by-blow account of the discussions – you should encourage him to write them more in the style of the action meeting, like this page here. Give him an idea of the other types though, because he may need to capture more information where there's an issue discussed which might be more complicated and have different stances.

OK, I can do a couple of checklists based on that. How about the agendas?

Well, you can always use some examples from previous meetings which you've run – and then give an idea of how you allocate time, how you deal with the minutes of the previous meeting, controlling discussion to stick to the subjects, what's covered by AOCB and so on .....

What does the "C" stand for? I usually just put "AOB".

They tend to say "Any Other Competent Business" nowadays – it gives you a way out by ruling things as not being competent or relevant!

Oh right – fair enough.

So, David looked out several agendas for a range of previous meetings he had chaired – a progress meeting (focusing on action statements), the monthly management meeting, a project meeting with clients and finally the Parish Community Council meeting (as he was a member of that committee in his home village). Although there were slight differences, especially with the Action List format for the progress meeting, there was a common structure repeated in them all.

STRUCTURE OF AGENDA

Specification of Meeting/Title

Time and location

1. Apologies advised by those who could not attend
2. Review of previous meeting minutes as being accurate
3. Any direct matters arising from this past meeting detail

4.1 Item 1

4.2 Item 2

etc

5. AOCB
6. Date (and location) of next meeting

Focus Time 7.2

If you were David and you had these resources (the general structure above and copies of the variety of Agendas), how would you use these in a championing session with Greg on the effective use of agendas? Think through a possible strategy now. If it helps, make some notes of these ideas separately.

Resource details

Reading through details from the handbook which Harry had provided, David extracted the key information, which he set down in a handout following the lines of the detail which follows:

Meeting Minutes

One of the benefits of having a good agenda – and sticking to it – is that the minutes of the meeting follow the same structure very closely. There's only one key addition to the structure – a note of all those who were present at the meeting – which comes after the opening details and before the list of those who have sent their apologies.

There are also different styles of writing minutes, from reported speech:
"Mrs Jones reported that she had arranged for the purchase of three new computers, at a total cost of ...."
to a briefer, general narrative style, as with:
"After a lively debate, it was agreed that the secretary should send a letter to the Council, outlining our key concerns as noted below."
What additional information might be useful in this type of handout?

Selecting the best training response for Greg

By using resources applying this type of information and referring to the agendas and minutes that were used for the meetings that Greg has watched, David could underline the way that good structure could help control the meeting.

When the two men started discussing this, it became obvious that Greg was not short of confidence or assertiveness – his problem was more that he wasn't sure of the structures and formats. He therefore felt slightly hesitant about controlling the progress and procedures positively. This was evidently why he wasn't being forceful.

So there was no need for him to go on an assertiveness training course.

On the subject of courses, Harry had discussed his needs with the training department and they'd recommended a one-day time management course that had one objective emphasising prioritisation and the progressing of actions towards completion – exactly the requirements that Greg had. So, he was booked to go on that, on the understanding that he would briefly discuss the outcomes and applications with David afterwards, as they applied to chairing meetings.

Action Time 7.3

Now that Greg is showing a bit more confidence, Harry has agreed to come along and help to facilitate his next Works Council meeting. The purpose of this is to make sure that the meeting progresses well, follows the agenda and keeps to time. This will reinforce the learning points that Greg has covered so far.
As an additional objective, Harry will be making sure that everyone gets a chance to speak and make a contribution during the meeting.
What are some of the key points that Harry might observe?
They might include:

- *Does Greg give an indication of the amount of time that can be spent on each Agenda item – and control it?*
- *Is he watching for people who wish to make a statement – and inviting them to speak if others are tending to "hold the floor"?*
- *Does he summarise progress periodically, to keep the meeting moving forward and encourage fresh input?*
- Is he reaching proper conclusions/outcomes at the end of each agenda item and establishing any follow-on actions before progressing to the following item?

So, the key issues which Greg hopes to address during this meeting – and which Harry is facilitating to make sure that they happen – include:

- the meeting keeps moving forward;
- conclusions and agreed outcomes are reached;
- discussions and member involvement are wide-ranging;
- control of time is maintained; and
- notes are made of the key detail discussed.

The intention here is that Greg will discuss his progress on these issues with David later – and Harry can compare notes with David regarding this progress and how David's championing programme should develop from that point onwards.

Action Time 7.4

Here are some of Harry's notes about Greg's "performance". Consider how you would discuss these with Greg if you were working with him, in order to encourage him to plan alternative strategies, while maintaining a positive attitude.

1. Still allowing some people to talk too long – while some others hardly speak at all.
2. Spent too long on agenda item two – still another four items to discuss.
3. Lost control a bit when Bill and Allan started arguing.
4. Had problems trying to explain the new schedule – need to plan a visual.
5. Moved on to agenda item four without closing off a conclusion/action for item three.

So, Greg has progressed quite a lot and has had a range of short coaching and mentoring experiences from both David and Harry, as his workplace champions.

Let's leave Greg for the moment – he still has his presentation planning meeting to experience – and let's think about how David's championing skills have progressed.

During the programme to date, David has been involved in:

- *identifying the learner's key problem areas;*
- *prioritising the key elements of the championing programme;*
- *identifying some different techniques which can be used;*
- *arranging for different development events for Greg;*
- *identifying "best practice" through discussion with Greg;*
- *preparing or accessing development resources for use;*
- *planning how to use these resources most effectively;*
- *identifying and responding to specific championing and training needs;*
- *monitoring the individual learner's attempts at practical consolidation; and*
- *facilitating and debriefing Greg's attempts at these workplace applications.*

So, with Harry's help, David has also been on a learning path – and has progressed well towards being a confident workplace champion.

There was one final learning area which Greg had to experience – the structure and planning involved in giving fairly formal presentations at his meetings, in order to get a lot of practical information across.

In order to experience this, Harry has arranged to take Greg to "sit in" at a planning meeting of one of his teams. This team, from the Procurements Department, are already highly motivated towards Harry's Workplace Development programme and have been progressing together as a close team, applying the holistic blending of individual strengths, for several months now.

As workplace champion and individual learner walk together along the corridor towards Meeting Room 5, Harry fills Greg in about some of the background – and the objective of the meeting they are about to observe.

The Presentation Planning Meeting

This is quite a young team but they're very enthusiastic. They've been asked to prepare a presentation for the Director (Denise) to set out a new policy that they want to happen in their department.

Right Harry. Do you think Denise will agree to them doing it if they manage to "sell" their message clearly?

Yes, I guess so. She just wants to make sure that they've thought the situation through properly. I've been involved with their discussions – and I think they've a good case .... so it's down to getting this presentation sorted.

It sounds a bit more complicated than I'll ever be doing with the Works Council.

It probably is – this is a team presentation involving several people – but you should get a lot of good ideas and you can adapt these to suit your needs. We can have a chat about them later.

OK

Here's the door. I think they've already started so, if we just quietly slip in the back of the room, we can listen to what they're discussing.

"So, where do we start then? Oh, hello Harry."

"Hi Margaret. This is Greg – remember, I said I'd bring him along to watch how it all happens. Don't mind us – we'll just sit quietly at the back."

"Hello Greg. OK folks. Have we figured out what we're trying to achieve with this presentation?"

"To impress Denise and get her to agree to our ideas."

"Let's keep things right and call her the Director – OK but let's be more specific. What do you expect her to be able to do – or know about – after hearing and seeing our presentation, that she couldn't before we started?"

"Oh ..... be able to select areas of our business that would be better done by outside contractors ....."

"With costings and such like – she'd need facts and figures to support the recommendations, wouldn't she?"

"Yes – and presumably also identify those we should carry on providing internally."

"Yes. How about Denise .... sorry, the Director being clear of the, you know, judgements we've used to decide these things?"

"The criteria – yes James, we should do that. And how can we check at the end of the presentation that the message has got across clearly?"
"She should be able to, in some way, list the areas we've identified – and explain the main ideas we've given for each."
"Yes – that sounds quite clear – use words such as 'list', 'identify' and 'explain', which show the kind of activity that would be involved."
"That's OK but how can we check she's remembered things? We can't give her a test – she'd hit the roof!"
"No, not a test – but we can make sure the key points come over clearly in the final summary – and check her understanding from the way she responds. We'll soon see from how the discussion develops, whether she agrees or not. Anything else we need to include?"
"Describe the benefits of using outside contractors?"
"Yes – and I suppose, to give balance, we should ....?"
"Review the benefits of using in-house providers, where that's being suggested."
"So these are all, loosely-speaking, objectives for our presentation – or its goals."
"Yes, let's write the different objectives on the flipchart. Then we can keep checking them as we progress with the design. It'll keep us on the track – make sure we don't start including stuff that's not important. Although, remember, they are guidelines. The plan might change .... and then we might have to change one or more of the objectives. But there would have to be a good reason!"
"Can we start designing our visuals now? I fancy doing some overhead transparencies. I'm good at art .... can I do the visuals?"
"Hang on Ed. We can't do them yet. We don't know the wording or pictures we need yet. No. What should come next ... anybody got any ideas?"
"Should we maybe list the main bits of information which we'll need to cover under each of these objectives you've written up there – list the key points, maybe?"
"Yes, good. So how can we do that? We need to have as many ideas and bits of information as possible, don't we?"
"How about having a brainstorming session – that usually gets the ideas out quickly."
"Right, so that'll get the information down on the flip-chart. Then what?"
"Sort them out under the main headings ...."
"Get them flowing logically ...."
"Now can we get on with the visuals?"
"Not yet, Ed. Here, take the pen – you can write things up on the flip-chart – that'll keep your artistry going! What do we have to do before starting on the visuals – Helen?"
"Well, we need to have sorted out the key points – the key statements. But even before that, we need to figure out how we're going to get the message across best."
"That's the visuals, surely?"
"Oh, shut up about the visuals, Ed."
"Yes. Getting the message across – the presentation techniques – such as ...?"
"Lecture, discussion, exercise ...."
"Visuals ...."
"Oh, for ...."
"No, Ed's right – if he means as a support for the presenter – or to summarise detail – or to present statistics ... visuals are a technique in their own right. Anything else?"

"We could have a list of the different services and functions in the company, and use that as a checklist or discussion prompt at the end. That would help people focus on the main choice, and make sure we didn't miss any out."

"OK. So far, we've sorted out the objectives; made a list of the key areas to be covered to meet each one; set out some of the details under each; thought through the techniques which we plan to use .... and drafted out the key prompt words or phrases and other illustrations which we need for the visuals. Any thoughts on these, Ed?"

"There's not much scope for pictures, probably. If we're thinking of using different presenters doing sections of the presentation, it'll look better if the visuals are done in a standard way. Maybe a little Departmental logo – the same colours used for headings .... stuff like that. It'll be mainly words, headings, statements .... Do you want to stick to using the overhead projector? I went on a short course on PowerPoint™ a while back but haven't had much chance to put it into practice. I can use it to design the masters for the projector acetates .... but what do you think about projecting a PowerPoint™ presentation instead of the overhead projector? I'm up for it!"

"If you're confident, certainly using PowerPoint™ could look better – more professional ... and we could get a bit of animation built in. I'll have to check if there's a media-projector to plug the laptop into. Good for you, Ed. It'll give you a bit of practice! Remember – keep the wording on the visuals as brief as you can."

"Yes, I'll stick to key phrases – not complete sentences. I'll even cut it down to single words where I can. So – how are we finally going to give the presentation?"

"I reckon that, seeing that Ed's so keen, he should do the whole thing – visuals, presentation ... the lot!"

"No way. This is a group presentation – we've all got to do our bit. I've got in first because I reckon that I'm quite good at doing the graphics and working the equipment and that kind of thing. But, the rest of you have got your own skills – at planning, answering questions, giving speeches .... come on you lot – what are you good at doing? Blow your own trumpets a bit – what are your strengths?"

"Yes – Ed's right. We've all got something we can give to the presentation. We may just need three or four people actually up front doing the talking, answering the questions and so on .... but there's the planning, producing documents .... and of course there's the visuals. Is everyone happy that Ed does them?"

"He'll just whine if we don't let him!"

"Just the same as you'll whine if you don't get to do some of the talking, Charlie. You are a member of the local Toastmasters' Society, after all."

"Maybe Charlie can act as sort of Master of Ceremonies or Chairman. It's good to have a link person, to keep things moving forward, introduce the different speakers, field the questions. Who else do we need for the actual presenting?"

"We need one person – maybe two – to go over the more detailed, technical stuff – someone who knows enough about the background to be able to answer the questions at the end fairly confidently as well."

"Sue's been involved in doing all the research and compiling the statistics ...."

"But I'm no use at speaking publicly – I just go to pieces!"

"Well, none of us really fancies standing up in front of the Director, given the choice."

"Charlie probably does, he's a masochist! How about if you're not up on your feet giving any of the actual presentation – but there up front to answer questions, Sue?"

"I don't mind that. I can cope with handling questions – I just don't think I'm the best choice for giving the actual presentation – some of you lot are much better at projecting and varying your voice and speaking confidently and all that stuff."

"Margaret and I can talk about the technical bits, if you like. We've been involved with the research too and we've both had a bit of practice talking to small groups in our slot during the Induction Training programmes."

"Fine, and Sue can help you sort out the detail at the planning stage. That leaves you and Gerry to write the documentation – that shouldn't be a problem for you two, with your past writing experience. So, I think that's everything. Yes, Charlie?"

"So, I'll do links ..... summarise the key points that have been made, bring in the next speaker – section of detail .... that kind of thing. I'll control the questions and feed them to Sue ..... or someone else if it's on a particular topic that they know better. And Ed, you liaise with them all to get the text for the visuals. Remember folks – the visuals take quite a long time to produce, so be fair and get your draft copies to Ed as soon as you can. I'll leave you to sort out deadlines, Ed."

"We'll need to practise all this."

"Of course. It's really important to practise the links of a group presentation – to make sure we have the flow and continuity. You told us that, didn't you Harry?"

"Yes – well done for remembering. You've got a maximum of thirty minutes for the whole thing, within the Board Meeting Agenda. That includes the time for questions – so you should work on the actual presentation lasting a maximum ...... and I mean maximum .... of twenty minutes. There's no point in over-running and then having no time to handle the questions, allowing you to sort out any opposition and doubts."

"We should be OK. There's one other thing though – let's think about the final question section for a moment."

"What happens if there aren't any questions?"

"It doesn't do any harm to finish early – better early than late! But there will be questions .... you can count on it!"

"You'll cope with the Director, won't you Sue!"

"It's not just Sue on her own. The whole team's there to help. Remember, support each other – we're all a team together. Charlie, you'll keep things moving, won't you? Think of yourself as a sort of Chairman, keeping things moving forward.

So, let's see now – we've got the objectives, the key points and the details to be included under each of these; we've figured out the different techniques we'll probably use .... and who's going to present the different bits. We've sorted out who's going to do the documentation ...."

"And we've got a Chairman or facilitator to keep things moving in line ..."

"... And he can keep an eye on the time, too. That's part of your job, Charlie."

"OK – but everyone must pay attention. It's no use me waving at someone to get them to finish off, if they just go blinding on regardless .... it spoils it for the others."

"That's fair enough – follow Charlie's lead, everybody. Remember to keep things in line during the planning and preparation stages as well. Keep asking – 'Is this relevant? Does it help to meet the objective? Is it a need to know or a nice to know?'"

"What do you mean by that, Harry? What's the difference?"

"The NEED TO KNOWS – you must include; the NICE TO KNOWS are valuable, but not so important – the illustrative example, Say. It's a kind of filter .... a measure of importance, especially if you're getting short of time.

Watch you don't overlap onto someone else's material, by mistake. That happens very easily sometimes, especially if you've practised your presentation a few times .... you start referring to other people's examples, or material, or even the detail that you've heard at rehearsal."

"Can I help to get the equipment organised – the overhead – or computer and the special projector, depending on what we use? I could help Ed produce the visuals as well. We've spoken, haven't we Ed and you'll show me a bit about how to use PowerPoint™. Will that be OK, Harry?"

"That's fine, Liam. Make sure that you discuss the detail – so that everyone's happy with the decision. Remember – it's them who'll be using the kit on the day, so do it the way they want!"

"This is looking good – and we haven't even got the main facts down on paper yet!"

I think we can leave them now, Greg – they'll be getting down to the detail of the content now. I think there's been quite a lot of helpful information in there though.

Yes, Harry – It's given me a lot of good ideas. Thanks.

Action Time 7.5

The team discussion which Harry and Greg (and you) have just listened to, covered a wide range of different criteria which should be applied when designing a presentation – whether a group presentation or one to be delivered by an individual.

Add to the following list of the key criteria covered, as it would apply to workplace championing –

- *Establish the purpose.*
- *Refine this as an objective (or statement of the expected outcome).*
- *Identify the key points.*
- *Plan the main detail to be included.*
- *Consider how to get the message across clearly.*
- *Include periodic activities and responses to keep the learner active.*
- *Think through how to round off the session and check understanding.*
- *Plan possible reinforcing activities to practise later in the workplace.*

8 The New Champion – Preparation

One-minute overview

In this chapter we'll focus on the preparatory activities involved in the process of workplace championing. These will include how the champion goes about final preparations, ensuring his/her own confidence by having support and backup in place. It also considers how the champion can plan strategies to build a rapport with the learner, develop benchmarks to check their own effectiveness and monitor the learner's current skill and knowledge levels.

So now we've reached our final section – the actual act of workplace championing. Working on the basis that you shall be involving yourself in these workplace development activities, we'll be concentrating on reinforcing the necessary skills, so that you'll be ready for action. You could of course be involved in delivering any given subject, so we won't be concerned with actual subject matter detail here. We're focused on the process – the actual activities involved in getting your championing message over successfully. You already know the content and are competent and proficient in your subject.

The individual and the big picture

In previous chapters, we've been concentrating on the philosophy behind our overall workplace development process. We've achieved this largely by following through the process itself. Now we'll be focusing on one person's involvement in the overall activities, viewed as a linear development.

However, we mustn't lose track of the fact that our model potentially involves a whole range of championing activities happening at the same time. This requires us to think on the two levels – of individual learner and workplace champion – at the same time. Picture a wide range of individual learners each at his or her own unique stage of development … and add to that a large group of workplace champions. As with the learners, each champion will be at a particular point on his/her progress in applied championing skills.

Of course, individual learners in one subject area can also be champions for another. This all creates what might be described as a complex and confusing spaghetti of developmental paths, woven loosely together. Let's try to get rid of the confusion by visualising it in a slightly more structured way.

Think of yourself as one of a whole group of workplace champions, in the process of developing your skills. Relax comfortably as you read the following – or better still, close your eyes and get someone else to read it to you.

Focus Time 8.1

Imagine that you're in the countryside, soaking in the peace, fresh air and relaxed atmosphere that's all around. You're standing on a grassy track, with fields around you and, as you look towards the skyline, you can see the track stretching off into the distance – a long straight track. Behind you, the track stretches backwards into the distance, representing the progress you have already made.

If you look to one side of the track, you can imagine a hedge – a hawthorn hedge – not too high but quite thick and spikey. You can see over this hedge to the fields beyond but it would be difficult to get through the hedge .... not impossible ... but difficult.

On the other side of the track, you see a fence, stretching off into the distance. Again, it's not too high and you may be able to picture an occasional stile, to allow you to cross at particular points.

These represent the boundaries of the track – the constraints or "ground rules" within which you operate – some legal, some moral, some personal, some imposed. The natural rules of order are represented by the hedges; the man-made legislation is indicated by the fence. These will normally define your decisions – although, if you're "thinking outside the box" to any degree, there is always the possibility of climbing over the fence or forcing your way through the hedge!

Imagine that you're now floating – looking down on this track. You may be able to see a series of milestones positioned along it. They're not really milestones, measuring miles – think of them as way markers, charting the many and varied goals which there are in this track which we travel through in life. And, looking even more closely, you'll see that the spaghetti of lines which we saw generally, in fact represents the paths that individuals are taking along the track. Each line is a unique trail – like a snail's trail along the garden path – marking the progress from one selected goal to the next. Each line represents the way that a particular developing champion has progressed, developing strengths, applying new and different techniques and learning new championing skills to apply with different learners, in different ways.

At the head of each line you may be able to see a tiny dot – perhaps you can see it as a spark of light .... of energy – representing that particular developing champion, taking that particular path. Sometimes, these different development paths will run side by side, with the potential for individuals helping each other. Occasionally lines may cross or obstruct each other, where there is perhaps a shortage of resources or where someone loses sight of the benefits of holistic co-operation.

Some dots are moving quite dynamically, while others have been static for some time. But all are moving forward to some degree, long-term.

It's probable that no two paths are incorporating exactly the same number and sequence of goals – it's likely that many of these champion sparks will also be learners at other times in their development process. So, sometimes the individual is developing by receiving help from other champions, as an empowered learner. At other times, s/he will be gaining experience as champion, through working with someone else. It makes the spaghetti a little more complicated but now that you can see each strand rather than a plate-full, everything is hopefully becoming clearer!

It takes organisation to keep all of these individual dots moving forward – but it also requires a strong degree of individual empowerment, with each workplace champion and each individual learner taking an active role in making the progress happen.

One of these sparks of energy represents you – charting your progress forward and indicating the choice of goals which still present themselves ahead. The hedges and fences represent the controls and constraints which direct your way forward – although you always have the conscious option of re-viewing out over the boundaries and making up your own mind.

There are always the stiles to consider – and also the option of pushing through weak points in the hedge, or climbing over the fence, if you feel strongly about your direction of personal progress! Just remember that the phrase "thinking outside the box" implies that you're pushing out against and through these boundaries. Stand by your principles!

Think about your goals; picture your path ahead; consider the parameters which you work within; review the possibilities for co-operation which exist with others; see the "bigger picture", holistic effect where people working together produce an extra, dynamic synergy as a result. Think about it!

Spend a few moments quietly identifying your own priorities – and deciding how you would wish to progress along your developmental path.

In your own time, focus on your slow breathing .... and gradually return to your normal state.

Seeing the way ahead

This type of visualisation can give you a real concept to imagine or even mentally picture, to see more clearly the way that people can develop and interact within a more holistic atmosphere. Progressively, we'll look in greater detail at some of the key criteria for building our more holistic working environment. At this stage, it may still appear slightly idealistic or theoretical. That's OK – it's only when you can actually experience such a synergy happening that you'll begin to realise the vast potential which is stretching off down our development track.

So, let's get down to the preparation.

Getting yourself ready for your first championing attempts

Preparation is important, to ensure that you can approach your first championing attempts confidently. If we build on the criteria which we've already established, we'll get closer to guaranteeing that they will turn out to be a success. Remember our SERIOUS champion?

S killed	-	in his/her championing competencies
E ffective	-	in use of time and learning outcomes
R eciprocal	-	the 360 degree championing goal
I nformed	-	about appropriate skills and techniques
O bjective	-	in both planning and decision making
U nified	-	in mission, message and techniques
S pontaneous	-	responding to needs as and when required

In establishing our foundation, we've been working on the basis that you have had some experience of training informally – or at least imparting information and knowledge to others. If not, you should make sure that you've really absorbed the detail of the earlier sections in this book, especially the sections relating to objective structuring and the different styles of presenting information.

It's crucial that you've totally absorbed the concept that any learning must be presented in phases, with each phase reinforced and its understanding by the learner checked before proceeding to the next stage .... bite-sized chunks, remember? And, having accepted the principle, your preparation must show that you can respond to it. One of the biggest potential traps for a workplace champion is to assume too much understanding on the part of the learner and present the detail as a continuous stream of new information. Regular checks, knowledge reinforcement and real examples are all crucial.

Society is increasingly becoming information and knowledge-led – we can find specific information on virtually anything, thanks to the internet. Within our workplace, we certainly have access to information relating to our areas of competency. Championing translates this base information into knowledge and practical competency, through the experience and skill of the champion.

The skills translation process

Championing doesn't necessarily involve a lot of pre-session preparation, teacher-style. Because you'll be working as champion on a subject about which you are fully conversant and in an environment in which you're comfortable, you already have everything you potentially need at your finger tips. The act of subdividing and sequencing information is in reality an action which encourages – or even forces – you to slow down, limit your expectations and not overload your individual learner with information. It will also ensure that you check understanding periodically – and give any additional remedial inputs necessary.

Remember the subdivisions:

Application

Understanding

Knowledge

Think in an objective way. Noting down your key learning objectives will help focus on the standards you want the learner to achieve – and the activities s/he'll have to carry out in order to achieve them. They don't have to be too detailed – at least think through the processes involved and establish an end point. This will indicate the sequence of learning points to work through, as well as producing a final check point to match achievement against. The more you consciously apply it, the more objective thinking will show itself to be a useful and effective tool.

Ask yourself questions, such as:

- What's my individual learner trying to achieve?
- How much can I expect him to absorb in a single learning session?
- Bearing in mind his current skill level, am I being reasonable?
- To reach this outcome, how do I subdivide the information?
- Could I cope with these "bite-sized chunks" if I was at his level?
- What activities will reinforce the understanding of these chunks?

Getting the starting level right

It's very easy, especially when working with a group of people, to assume too much – to assume too high a starting level, too great an ability to assimilate the new information, or expecting too great an ability to handle large amounts of new information at too fast a speed.

Remember, it's safer to ASSUME NOTHING.

This doesn't mean you must start from scratch on every occasion – it does however mean you should check on what the individual learner's comfortable starting point will be and then design the learning around that level. Having over-high expectations can almost become a defence mechanism on our part as champions (as it can also happen with trainers and coaches). We don't want to repeat old stuff they already know – so err towards the other extreme. We potentially expect too much prior knowledge, begin too high and too fast ..... and lose them from the start! There's really no excuse for doing this as a workplace champion. You're working one-to-one with your learner – who you want to empower to be an active participant in the design as well as the implementation of the learning ... so ask and discuss!

On the subject of consolidation, there's a difference between repetition and reinforcement – repeating the same thing several times is demotivating – almost insulting. Reinforcing the information through additional information is very valuable: by giving an example, describing a scenario which illustrates the information or discussing how your individual learner might become involved in applying the ideas directly within the workplace, for example.

The benefits of one-to-one championing

When you're working consciously with your learner on a one-to-one basis, you'll automatically be more closely aware of his/her level, pace and need for reinforcement. Through regular questioning, listening and observation, you'll also be able to spot when there's any confusion or blockages – and be able to respond immediately to get the individual learner back on track again. Establishing levels of understanding and formulating clear questions don't necessarily come easily to everyone, so prior thought and planning can help. Try asking questions – then checking that it's clear **exactly** what you're requiring as detail in the answer. It's sometimes harder than it sounds – if the individual learner's concentrating effort into trying to figure out what you're asking, s/he's got less brain power remaining to provide the detail you think you've requested!

How assured support and backup encourages confidence

Remember the integrated triangle – the individual learner at the top, the workplace champion in the lower left corner ... and development support in the remaining corner. Each corner relates to the other two in a dynamic trinity. The following exercise illustrates one of my favourite images, illustrating this dynamic.

Focus Time 8.2

Think of your thumb and first two fingers, positioned so that the three tips make the corners of a triangle.

Place an elastic band round these fingers, up near the fingertips, to make a triangle.

Move your fingers around, bringing two tips close together, then the other two and so on. This represents when the champion and learner are working closely together at times, while at other times, the champion and support function might be shown as co-operating closely. Whenever two representative corners are integrating, they still have a dynamic effect on the third corner of the triangle – the action of the elastic band. So –

- *the support function is providing resources for the champion to use with the individual learner;*
- *the effectiveness of champion and individual learner working together will be affected by the quality of overall support;*
- *the individual is creating the resource requirements being discussed by the champion and support function; and*
- *the champion's delivery techniques will make or break the success of the material supplied by the support function (DSF).*

Now slip the finger representing the support function out of the elastic band relationship. The champion and learner are still relating together but can be too distant at times, while at other times they come together, head-to-head. The dynamic is spoiled. The joint co-operation requires support.

The moral of this illustrated tale is that resource support is extremely important for the successful operation of the workplace championing process. If your development session requires supporting materials, it's very important that these are available when you need them – and that you can use them confidently.

Focus Time 8.3

As a learning facilitator, I often use PowerPoint™ presentations, requiring both a computer and a media projector to operate. It's a relatively high-tech approach, which will only work effectively if all equipment, leads and software are present and correct. I suspect many of us have experienced such presentations where something went wrong – or the difficulties of having to operate the technology was distracting the presenter from relating directly to the audience.

To cover the eventuality of something going wrong, I usually bring a duplicate set of overhead projector (OHP) acetates as a backup. I might also bring a handout of the reduced PowerPoint™ screens (which can easily be printed off), in case the OHP breaks down as well – but that's really anticipating the worst case scenario. One way or another, at least I know that I've got the resources to allow me to get my message across. This helps my confidence, before and during the event.

Confidence is Key

If it requires this level of backup support to make the trainer rest easy and feel confident, it's well worth the extra effort. The same is true for one-to-one workplace championing activities. If you, for example, find it difficult to remember formulae or definitions, you'll feel more confident in the knowledge that you have a handout, check sheet or visual aid setting this detail down for reference during the session. The same would be true with having a process flow diagram to discuss, if you had doubts about presenting the sequence of events accurately. It is, after all, the detail and your experience which is important – not remembering mnemonics and other supposed memory aids, if you find it difficult to remember what the letters stand for!

Ask for and expect support

Part of the integrated triangle participant agreement (see page 116) is that, if you're going to give your time to help with informally developing others, you must be in the position to expect direct assistance in accessing the support resources you require. This is the role of the development support function (DSF), which encompasses senior management and other specialist departments, as well as HR and Training.

Expect this support – and make sure you ask for and receive it.

Know thyself

If anyone knows about you – you do! Things like:

- the activities which give you a real "buzz";
- the skills which you will never be totally at ease with;
- the techniques you prefer to use, to get the message across;
- the little, secret biases you might have against certain people;
- the responses and attitudes which wind you up;
- your level of ability to see things in a linear, objective way;
- your expectations of people, working for the general good;
- your personal priorities and identified development needs;
- your working relationships with other decision-makers; and
- your capability at controlling and managing your time.

Action Time 8.1

Think about these for a few moments – really think about them.

Make some separate notes to help you sort out your own piece of "developmental spaghetti" – you don't need to share these with others ... it's really more a case of clarifying your own ideas, priorities and goals.

- *This will help you see your own way forward, identifying your own key areas.*
- *It will also help you see the key strengths you should be developing further as a workplace champion.*

As a part-time coach/mentor/tutor, you only have so much time to devote to the overall championing process. Be realistic. The more you've clarified the guidelines in your head and the more confident you are about the overall "mechanics" of the operation prior to starting, the faster you can switch from doing your normal work to becoming an active workplace champion.

Building a rapport with your learner

Once the programme is up and running, it's quite possible you could be working with several learners, potentially in different subject areas, around the same period of time (remember that spaghetti along the track!).

For ease of reference, we'll concentrate on one. As with working out your CPD using a personal planning system such as ID Plan, once you've focused on completing one development track from start to finish, the others then follow a similar and easier-to-complete pattern.

Learning tends to be like that – the first attempts are slow and rather laborious, until you get the hang of it and put your ideas into practice. Once you've practised the principles once or twice, you gradually get faster and more confident. This is why it's important to select our first few championing activities carefully, to give a greater guarantee of this growth of confidence.

We're using that: – Knowledge – Understanding – Application – continuum again!

Everyone's welcome at the party!

As we've established totally by now, our integrated model of workplace development involves everyone, at all levels. Seniority is not an issue in the equation – what is important is the communication of knowledge, experience and skills to where it's required, from where it already exists (and is being applied competently). Remember the creative consistency within the seven Cs –

- Competent
- Consistent
- Conversant
- Credible
- Creative
- Communicative
- Co-operative

Creative Consistency

Maintain the status quo. Work on the basis of the "if it ain't broke, don't fix it" principle. Allow people's confidence to grow in the knowledge that the ground rules are understood and maintained by all. But, at the same time, encourage imagination and right brain thinking. Consider improvement and expansion – but not change simply for its own sake. Apply creative thinking within the bounds of the known development track.

Interpersonal Skills

Does it make a difference to you whether you're speaking to someone in a position senior to you – or whether they're junior to you in the hierarchy? It often depends to some extent on the way the hierarchy operates. If you have a management that rules dictatorially, it might be more of a problem. Here the "superior" might feel uneasy being championed by a subordinate, perhaps seeing it as a public display of weakness and therefore a threat to authority.

Because of this attitude, setting up such a workplace championing arrangement might present added difficulties in this type of vertically managed environment. To get things started correctly, it's important that we select champion/learner pairs who will function positively together. Their interaction then sends out the correct signals.

Responding to particular situations

Alternatively, to get the system operating, an outside consultant can be brought in as champion for individual senior requirements. A half-way house where the consultant acts more as facilitator, supporting an internal champion, can also be an initial way forward. This can certainly get the development atmosphere sorted out and the preliminary hang-ups overcome.

Flat hierarchies

For the purpose of our exercise, let's think more positively and currently and consider the development of workplace championing relationships in a more horizontal hierarchy. The status issue will be less of a consideration, so we can focus on other matters. Let's think about some of the key points to review when setting up each workplace development relationship. Here are a few questions to ask yourself.

Action Time 8.2

1. *What is my current working relationship with this potential individual learner?*
2. *What do I have to do to relate to this individual as an equal colleague?*
3. *Which common interests do we have which I could use to "break the ice"?*
4. *How much do I know about his/her current level of knowledge and skill in the area?*
5. *How aware am I of his/her ability to understand and respond to new information?*
6. *If I'm aware of any hang-ups, what can I do to respond to them positively?*
7. *How might I set up the learning environment to make our interaction easier?*
8. *If there's a benefit in meeting socially to discuss the ground rules – how?*
9. *Is there anything I must do to prepare myself for the relationship? If so, what?*
10. *What are the key issues I must prepare myself for, before our first meeting?*

You may think of other questions, especially when you're considering a particular individual rather than this more general approach. The key point is, the more you can think through the situation beforehand – and review possible strategies – the more prepared you are to cope with eventualities ... and the more confident you'll feel.

Applying consolidation

We've already established the importance, when delivering learning to others, of regular stages of consolidation – recapping, reviewing, application .... it's the concept of establishing "bite-sized chunks" once more. Although we can use different names for the activity, the important issue is more that you're regularly injecting opportunities to discuss and sort out any confusions or misunderstandings which have arisen. In this way, both champion and individual learner can address problems at an early stage and keep the structure progressing forward on firm foundations.

Two-way communication between champion and learner

This principle is as important in workplace development as it is in general training. Part of developing a rapport with your learner will be sensing (and checking) how well s/he is following you and whether s/he has any queries which require further discussion. As you'll usually be working one-to-one, this shouldn't be a problem. If you're conscious of the person – and you must be – you'll see when they are confused or having doubts. The frown, the puzzled look, the hesitant attempt to ask a question, the progressive lack of response .... different people flag up their doubts in different ways. Part of getting to know each individual learner will therefore be finding out his/her particular responses and reactions. Better still, create an atmosphere where you're checking understanding as well as encouraging the learner to ask, unprompted, for further explanation when s/he requires it. If you can do this, you'll be largely eliminating the need for puzzled expressions in the first place!

Practical reinforcement as a key element of consolidation

One of the other key benefits of on-site or workplace championing is the potential for direct follow-up practice. Whereas a delegate on a general training course normally, on walking out of the training room door, loses direct contact with his/her trainer, you as a workplace champion are more likely to be a departmental colleague. In this role, you'll be on hand to answer any supplementary questions and arrange practical reinforcement as part of the day-to-day work of the department.

This is a key element of consolidation, reinforced further by the fact that integrated champion involvement within the department can be targeted totally at the needs, priorities and processes present in that department. This makes both the learning and the reinforcement absolutely relevant to the department's priorities ... which has got to be a key selling point in favour of Championing! We'll review the practicalities of reinforcement and consolidation in chapter ten. At this stage, we're more concerned about planning and setting up the exercises to make sure they're relevant. If they are, they're guaranteed to reinforce the learning points which have been the focus of previous development sessions. Get the planning right and the rest will follow!

Developing the championing relationship

Developing this relationship is important – it's something which the company should encourage through team development and co-operative working initiatives, rather than merely leaving it to individual champions. That's another of the roles for Development Support. But it does ultimately come down to how each champion behaves and the degree to which he involves himself in the overall process. It's also down to the amount of empowerment and involvement which the individual learner adds to the equation. It's up to each individual learner to take an active role in progressing their own development. By doing this, they are more likely to get the learning that suits them best.

Being a "buddy"

Of course, as with personal as well as business working situations, some relationships will work better than others. You can, after all, work with someone without being particularly close. However, a degree of flexibility and understanding does help create the atmosphere where learning can progress at a deeper level.

Time management is important in this championing context. While you don't want to be regularly interrupted during day-to-day work, or expected to drop what you're doing to sort out any problems which your learner may be experiencing, some degree of "rapid response" will be very helpful. This will be especially true in the early stages when your individual learner is trying to reinforce his/her learning in the workplace. This is where the spirit of co-operation is ripe for development.

This awareness will be fostered further if those acting as champions are also concurrently in the situation of being individual learners, coached and mentored by others. An element of "do as you would be done by" then enters the equation. As a learner yourself, you will be aware that you, for example, have become in the past totally "stuck" trying to get a particular computer function to operate. It may be that you only required a quick five minute reinforcement session to get you going again, because your champion made him/herself available. And indeed, these types of informal buddy inputs are going on every day.

Being realistic about the time for learning

The individual learner shouldn't expect an instant response if it's evident that the champion's concentrating on writing a report, or engaged in a similar cerebral activity. In this situation, being interrupted would break the concentration flow and subsequently waste the champion's time in getting back up to speed again. Using common sense, the learner can select a time to link up with the champion at a later, mutually convenient time, when both can concentrate on the development discussion.

This is part of the developing rapport which champion and learner would be seeking to develop. It's also encouraging the learner to think more pro-actively. On occasions where there is a question and the champion is unavailable, the individual as empowered learner can put some effort into actively finding answers him/herself.

Developing benchmarks to check your own effectiveness

Companies go through benchmarking exercises; national bodies expend large sums of money reviewing "best practice" and producing case studies of companies which we can all use as models to aspire towards. With these and other established standards firmly in your sights, you can of course identify your own benchmarks – and consider the steps and stages which you will need to take to progress towards their ultimate achievement.

Markers along the track

This ties in neatly with the concept of your personal marker stones or goals linking your individual path along the long straight track, as we visualised earlier in this chapter (that's the pile of spaghetti, remember!). Although "benchmarking" sounds rather grand and scientific, we can think of the activity as establishing your mutually agreed working levels or competencies, with the selected sequence of stepping stones you'll have to negotiate to ultimately reach these levels. It's perhaps less impressive-sounding but it's an easier idea to visualise.

It's important to realise that achieving a benchmark is not the end of the story, however. Where everyone is aspiring to achieve the same benchmark level, this means that, at best, everyone finishes up being average – at the same level. Using entrepreneurial imagination can raise you beyond the general benchmark level. It's called seeking the competitive edge!

Remember Creative Consistency. We're not pursuing change for its own sake – but we are looking to apply lateral imagination to make our performance different .... to improve upon the established benchmark. We do this consciously and with a particular outcome in mind, to allow ourselves and others to judge the increased success of our actions against any existing benchmark.

Identifying these benchmarks

So, how do we manage to define development benchmarks accurately?

Some will be specified for us. When you go through a company appraisal, your key goals for the following six months, year or whenever will be discussed. And make sure you do discuss them – appraisals should be a two-way process. If you've managed to think through your own goals and aspirations, you should be in a better position to talk about the realities of achieving the goals ... and making sure that some of the potential blocks you foresee can be reduced or even eliminated. One way or the other, you'll finish up applying these "official" benchmarks – you can be sure others will be checking your progress directly against them.

The added ingredient – extra dynamism

Hopefully, they'll be capable of appreciating any additional dynamism you've brought to the activity, to give your personal, extra "take" on its achievement. Credible creativity. Remember the long straight track with the fence and hedge – it's always ultimately possible to jump the fence or push through the hedge, if you really feel that's the best way forward! A word of caution, however – know your manager .... and the extent to which s/he sees lateral, innovative thinking as a positive factor. Some see rules and barriers as all-important, never to be breached!

Maintain the strength of your own convictions, however, as far as you can. Keep an eye on opportunities which extend beyond the normal boundaries of your development track. If it seems beneficial, do your best to incorporate such activities within your portfolio.

Setting your own benchmarks

Throughout this book, you've been responding periodically to a sequence of ***Focus Time*** and ***Action Time*** exercises which should have helped you identify your own development requirements – and the preferred standards that you should be aspiring towards achieving. See them as a form of personal competency check, linking with the benchmarks required by your working environment. For your personal workplace development activities, they'll come under a range of headings.

Action Time 8.3

Spend some time thinking through the range of headings you'll need, to establish your own set of benchmarks. Think wide – not deep. You're trying to capture the range of competency areas which are important for you, in order to become an effective champion. Let's start with a few, to set you thinking –

1. *Identification of key subject areas to be offered.*
2. *Ability to relate to particular shortfall needs of the individual learner.*
3. *Capability to respond directly to individual's learning and communication levels.*
4. *Awareness of the subdivisions of learning, as inputs and practical consolidation.*
5. *Ability to relate learning and reinforcement to the specific needs of the department.*

As with all competency benchmarks, you'll be closer to achieving some than others – indeed you may already have achieved some of those identified.

Competencies and benchmarks

This is a key area which the HR/Training World generally still hasn't quite got round to applying properly. We speak about competency levels and, particularly in areas of structured and open learning, we incorporate pre- and post- testing. The idea generally is that the trainer gives someone a pre-test before they study a particular subject. Let's say that the learner performs badly in some sections of this test – but answers other sections correctly. If the programme incorporates separate modules, the trainer can select the related subject modules where the learner has displayed lack of competency. The individual learning event is thus designed to suit that particular learner's development needs.

Using this process, the individual's learning programme includes only the learning modules where extra input is required – while eliminating areas where the learner has confirmed competency. This is certainly best practice but, in reality, ease of training event management and administration often dictates that the learner still experiences the complete learning event. This means that the learner is spending time reviewing sections of information which s/he has already proved him/herself to be competent at achieving. This is both demotivating and time-consuming.

One-to-one development, as applied in workplace championing, gives us a much stronger platform for identifying and specifically responding to individual competency deficiencies. This both reduces frustration and saves time – and can evidently be more effective than the "one size fits all" approach of conventional training.

Identifying competency levels holistically

So, part of our holistic approach to learning is the belief that people are already competent at some levels of skill and knowledge achievement. Following this belief, a pre-test might therefore be used to identify the particular areas in which a learner has demonstrated competency, as well as those which need to be developed further.

There's no need to waste time repeating the learning associated with the areas where competency has already been proved. A brief recap will usually be enough. Instead, the championing sessions focus on the sub-standard areas, identified through the pre-tests. The final reinforcement exercises will benefit from incorporating all areas, giving consolidation for both new and existing knowledge and skills.

We thus combine new with existing elements of competency, creating a positive, motivated result due to the individual becoming immersed in the overall value of the new learning. The end result, further enhanced by relevant, responsive workplace reinforcement, gives an overall effect which far exceeds the sum of the individual learning inputs. That's holistic synergy!

The reality of needs analysis

So, the real purpose of any activity designed to find the individual learner's initial competency level in any particular subject area, is to be able to use this information positively. Information gained must be used to develop learning which progresses from this point (once confirmed) rather than starting with the repetition of already known material. We must motivate the learner, rather than damping his/her enthusiasm by starting the learning experience by repeating detail that s/he already knows and is competent in practising.

If we can show that we are focusing on each learner's particular levels and needs and are responding positively and progressively to them, the rapport which we have been describing as being all-important is more likely to happen.

How competent are you?

An objective awareness of your own levels of competency will help to rationalise your development plans and encourage your personal motivation. In turn, this will help to refine and revise the sequence of benchmarks which you are gradually amassing. It's important that you are objectively clear about your own competencies – by establishing your own strengths and shortfalls.

Some will find it difficult to maintain objectivity when reviewing their own capabilities. Some may feel that there are political agendas afoot within their workplace, which could abuse an open admission of lack of competency in a particular subject area. Sadly, in the current atmosphere, this can still be the case, given the variability of management professionalism. This may well reflect on the degree to which you broadcast your personal findings to others – however, it should not reflect on your decision to carry out your own personal competency benchmarking, to assist in your own personal development planning. Just watch how (and more importantly, to whom) you broadcast these ideas in detail, until you're confident that the necessary attitudes, awareness and managerial objectivity are all in place!

Focus Time 8.4

As well as the visualisation of the winding individual path along the long straight track of personal development, I've another mental picture which I use to help workshop delegates see their own "Big Picture". It's the concept of kite flying. Have you ever been in a place where communal kite flying is happening? It could be in London's Hyde

Park – or on the Southern Downs – or on a beach somewhere. You may have seen films of the kite festivals in China.

It's this image of many kites tugging at their strings in the wind, captive but energised, which I want you to imagine. Focus on particular kites and what do you see? Some are spiralling madly, desperate to fly off if given the opportunity; others are hanging languidly in the air, maintaining their height but not doing very much. Some others will be gradually sinking to the ground, due to lack of inspired handling or even lack of attention.

Applications

If you're clear of your own competencies, your future requirements and the path and possible goals that you hope to achieve, you can use the kites' analogy to set up and keep your personal future progress in motion. Through it, you can identify –

- the activities which you want to develop further;
- the possibilities which are available to you;
- the priority issues – and others held for the future;
- the latent opportunities which are no longer of interest; and
- the areas where additional energy is necessary.

Planning systems such as I D Plan, mentioned previously, are good vehicles to use to register both your priorities and your progress. This brings reality and purpose to your personal benchmarking – and helps you maintain a focus on the way forward for future workplace championing activities, as well as your overall development plans.

Basically, here's how it works.

Case study – Darren's potential development

In Action Time 8.3 above, you established your key competency areas for being an effective workplace champion – and further identified those where you needed input to achieve a personal benchmarked level. So you should now be clearer about the key areas where you personally need further input and involvement.

For the sake of illustration, let's take two particular areas which a hypothetical champion, Darren, might need to develop further. We'll take these as:

1. learning more about what is involved in developing support resources; and
2. gaining more experience in relating to individuals one-to-one.

In reality, we would be more fully aware of his likely workplace requirements, current competency levels and future intentions. At this basic exercise level, taking the first heading as a reference point, we can establish that Darren might have particular goals to achieve, covering areas such as:

Area 1.

- be aware of the contents of any resource library currently available;
- know how to design and write effective checklists and exercises;

- find rapid ways of setting up practical learning experiences for learners; and
- establish ways of checking learner levels before and during sessions.

Keeping his eyes and ears open, Darren might hear about various opportunities and activities going on and could start "flying his kites". These activities might include –

- sending off letters and emails suggesting involvement;
- requesting detail and/or assistance;
- networking with others involved in the activities;
- reading related articles in magazines and newspapers; and
- identifying future contacts.

Some activities will receive almost immediate response, giving Darren concrete leads and activities to follow up; others may not receive any response initially but instead hang around in the air until some future activity suddenly makes them active. At this point, Darren might receive a phone call or receive notice of some conference or whatever, because he has been put on a mailing list as a result of his earlier contact.

And finally, undoubtedly, some of Darren's approaches will threaten to fall to the ground unanswered. If some issues are important to Darren, he might feel the need to give a tug at the string periodically (a follow-up phone call or email, a word in the right ear etc) to get things moving again. He'll probably just forget about some of the others, allowing them to sink into oblivion, inactive and unheeded.

Focus Time 8.5

So, what ideas might Darren focus upon, in relation to the four development areas identified under Area 1? They might include:

- *a telephone call to the guy in charge of the resource library;*
- *responding to details of a resources exhibition/conference in London;*
- *leaving a voice mail for a manager who has written some check sheets;*
- *speaking to an experienced workplace champion in the department;*
- *making a request for a book which got a good review in the newsletter;*
- *contacting a teacher/lecturer who has a good reputation for one-to-one;*
- *asking for a copy of a professional journal with a relevant article;*
- *meeting someone involved in writing structured open learning;*
- *contacting a technical college lecturer, involved in practical training;*
- *finding details of a book which relates learning objectives to outcomes; and*
- *making a request to sit in on a practitioner's practical training event.*

In various different ways, these will help our champion – Darren – to see the benefits of using a more structured approach, give him various opportunities to discuss real situations with people who have had relevant direct experience and expand his repertoire of ideas and techniques. They can all help to refine his competency at key related activities and establish personal benchmarks for future monitoring and development.

Identifying current skill and knowledge levels

Finally, after spending some time considering the new champion's competency levels and methods of responding to these, let's close the chapter with some thoughts on the skills involved when the champion is identifying competency levels for his individual learner(s). Like we said with the flying kites analogy, the principle's the same, whether you're doing it for yourself or for others.

The key to being able to do this effectively is having a clear awareness of the progression of learning, which we spent some time discussing in the initial chapters of this book. Remember, this progression links with established learning objectives, where the building blocks start with Knowledge, advance through Understanding and then reach the reinforcement stage of Application. As an example –

Application – The learner writes and discusses the outcomes of learning objectives.

Understanding – The focus and direction which a stated objective can present. ↑

Knowledge – How to write an objective – the important of actions and standards.

If we maintain our awareness of this Knowledge – Application sequence of development, we'll find it easier to position any learner on their appropriate point along the sequence. They may, for example, know the definitions and some of the theory but lack the practical (application) experience. In this scenario, after a quick recap of the basics, the championing session would focus rapidly on the practical application.

It's a case once more of identifying individual paths connecting the selected milestones on our overall learning track.

Action Time 8.4

So, again generalising rather than taking any particular subject area, you should be able to ask yourself the following questions about your learner's competency level.

These are separated into the three levels (Knowledge, Understanding and Application).

Knowledge

basic definitions, names of component elements, foundation information

Understanding

explanation of different components, description of functions, relationship of items

Application

examples of the complete process, practical illustrations, discussion of strategies

Ask yourself –

- *Is he aware of the terminology used?* (K)
- *Does he know the names of the component parts?* (K)
- *Is he clear of the progressive steps of any operation?* (K)
- *Can he identify the equipment required for the operation?* (K)
- *Is he able to describe and explain all the above?* (U)
- *Can he relate the activity or operation to other similar ones?* (U)
- *Can he explain how he will use his new competency at work?* (U)
- *Can he describe why some techniques etc must be used?* (U)

- *Can he demonstrate the sequence in the correct order?* (A)
- *Is he meeting the criteria and standards he has described?* (A)
- *Is he including all the safety and procedural issues described?* (A)
- *Is he progressively completing this activity more confidently?* (A)

Notice the progression moving up through the ***K****nowledge,* ***U****nderstanding and* ***A****pplication levels. It should be possible, through checking, to identify the particular level that any given learner has reached. Workplace championing on a one-to-one basis allows us to focus on the particular stage of learning for each individual, saving time and eliminating demotivation through repetition.*

Finding the starting and progression points

So, if our individual learner is clear about the equipment and basic (knowledge) stages of operational procedure involved in an activity (and has proved this to our satisfaction), our starting point would probably be to discuss (his understanding of) the detail and reasons behind the procedure and any safety, supply and other considerations associated with it.

We would then progress to talking through, then demonstrating, the (application of the) process. These activities have moved us on from the initial stage of Knowledge, checking that knowledge, to involvement in the Understanding level. This in turn has developed from initial theoretical input to practical demonstration by the champion.

The next stage would then involve the individual learner in trying to progress through the stages of the activity, initially focusing on each element separately if necessary, ensuring that all the standards and criteria are met. Through practise, this would gradually link together, become more fluid and progress to become the complete, though slowly executed activity.

These are all elements of the Application stage – which will gradually speed up (while maintaining competency/quality standards) until the learner can ultimately achieve output standards. These will be stated in any production objective as items produced per unit of time – or in a knowledge objective as incorporating and meeting the particular, specified standards. These different levels tie in very closely with the more formally stated progressive levels of behavioural learning objectives – understand these and you'll be able to build the framework upon which learning and competency can gradually evolve.

9 The New Workplace Champion – Checklist for Action

One-minute overview

This chapter starts with consideration of a championing contract agreement. It then looks at various examples of planning and preparing for championing events (both knowledge and practical-based) with the detail required for the specified stages. It considers the importance of resource provision and the revised role of development support – and the benefits of building co-operation through these activities. It reviews some of the specifics for championing, including questioning techniques and session planning, illustrating these with short case study examples.

So, the theoretical planning is in place – you've identified your individual learner; you've established his/her starting level and you've clarified the particular outcome (or objective) and competency level you're aiming for. The foundations are firmly established and you, as workplace champion, are ready to progress. This is when the prior preparation makes the actual learning session flow more easily (and confidently).

All sides of the bargain: what is expected from everyone involved

Earlier, we spoke about having some form of championing contract or agreement, to establish what could be expected from whom – and set out how the integrated triangle model functions in reality. We've reached the point in your preparations where the dynamic functioning of these relationships becomes very important. If you don't get the support you expect, it would be perfectly understandable if you (as workplace champion) decided to give up on the whole idea and walk away from it.

It's likely that there's nothing in your job description stating that you have to be involved in these types of coaching and mentoring activities to any degree. You're presumably becoming involved because you think it's a good idea and you can see the benefits which everyone can gain from it. It is, however, crucially important that everyone co-operatively "sings from the same hymn sheet" – and that does include ***everyone*** – at all levels in the organisation.

So, let's set something down in print which explains the parameters and expected integration. Consider it as a type of contract that everyone involved is signing up to – and can refer to as development progresses, if there are any blocks to the progress. These types of agreements, involving signed commitment, are quite common in business nowadays, to encourage long-term consistency in supporting any initiative. If things are really working co-operatively and holistically, you can of course probably progress happily without any contract. Do consider having one where there are any doubts remaining about the quality of on-going support and enthusiasm which may exist naturally. It's another technique for keeping the motivation moving forward.

Focus Time 9.1

The Integrated Triangle – Workplace Champion Agreement

This is an arrangement incorporating the trio of representative parties – the individual learner, the workplace champion and the support function (providing resources and organisational support). It establishes the relationship between these roles – which will apply to any particular "chunk" of development. The overall purpose is to encourage long-term support and motivation for the championing process.

This agreement is intended to set parameters in the early stages of developing championing strategies. Any individual can be ***workplace champion*** *for one subject area – while becoming the* ***individual learner*** *where s/he in turn needs a particular subject input. Additionally, someone providing* ***development support*** *for other champion/learner activities could become a learner or champion in their own right. Everyone can potentially have one of the three roles at any given time, for a specific learning area. This is represented in the model by the concept of "360 degree championing".*

The responsibilities and key involvement areas for the three parties are:

INDIVIDUAL LEARNER

- Take an active part in identifying personal strengths and shortfalls.
- Prioritise key personal goals to best match the needs of the business.
- Assist in focusing precisely on particular development needs.
- Take an active part in assisting the champion to arrange learning events.
- Seek out and apply workplace opportunities to reinforce completed learning.

WORKPLACE CHAMPION

- Relate to learner, in order to establish rapport and learning etc levels.
- Establish precisely, with learner's input, the key development objectives.
- Plan, in outline, how these objectives can be achieved and reinforced.
- Establish workplace championing events – in manageable "chunks".
- Set up longer-term learning reinforcement contact with learner.

DEVELOPMENT SUPPORT

- Respond to champion requests for information, assistance and advice.
- Source or produce basic resources to meet key established objectives.
- Assist with any background organisation and support required by champion.
- Act as central broker to manage and support championing strategies.
- Provide technique support role to develop the champion's skills.

We, the undersigned, acknowledge the importance of maintaining positive progress, both to allow the individual to function more dynamically – and to illustrate the benefits of workplace championing to others who may be considering its use.

We also agree to discuss any situations where the three-way co-operation is in danger of stalling, to resolve problems and permit championing to progress again.

Signed

Individual Learner..

Workplace Champion ....

Development Support Representative ....

Date ..../.... /.....

COPY AND RETAIN FOR REFERENCE

Getting ready for action: preparing for actually running the event

In the previous chapter, we spent some time working through the process of focusing specifically on:

- who our learner is;
- how specifically s/he needs to develop;
- what particular detail we need to cover;
- which possible technique(s) would be preferred; and
- what indicators we'll build in to check competency.

This was all at the planning stage – figuring out in overview how you'll plan to deliver the individualised learning. Now you're ready to prepare for and actually run the event. Once again, it perhaps requires emphasising that we're not considering your involvement as being that of a stand-up trainer, presenting information. You'll usually be working on a one-to-one basis with a single individual learner, so you'll really have the opportunity to be aware of and work at his/her level and pace ... and you'll have no excuse for losing him/her because you're blinding him/her with science or jargon, or expecting too much, too quickly.

The beauty of workplace championing is the potential for easily building a two-way relationship, allowing rapport to really develop – so take the time to make it happen.

Getting closer to starting off

We'll keep to general principles, so we're not considering specific subject areas here. What we can do is consider the workplace championing involvement for both a factual, knowledge-type of event and a more practical one.

- For any knowledge-type of event (such as learning about a new process or procedure), your main thrust initially will probably be to explain information relating to the particular subject – commonly-used terminology, key components, names, participants, definitions, titles and so on.
- The next stage will be to help the learner understand what these words actually mean and the theory behind how they can be made to apply within a work context.

Planning for a knowledge-based session

This activity involves referencing and discussing information, remember.

Champion and learner are likely to be sitting side by side, with some form of visual aid to focus on. This could be –

- a text book
- a single illustration
- a checklist of definitions
- a handbook explaining a technique

It's important that these are expressed in user-friendly ways. A standard operational procedure document is rarely written at the level of the new user and will undoubtedly require "translation", to make it understandable at the championing stage of development.

Most of the resources will be some form of printed word or illustration, which can be used as a reference point for discussion. Some will already be prepared or available in books and publications. Where nothing appropriate exists, some supporting resource may have to be produced.

Resources take time to find – and even longer to produce. This is why it's important to think about what's required at the planning stage, prior to the actual championing event. This is where the support function can (and must) come to the champion's aid. However, let's first consider our parallel practical type of event.

Planning for a practical session

Practicals usually involve activity – although some may well have an initial theoretical session (cementing the knowledge/understanding before progressing to the next stage of application). To ensure this practical reinforcement, equipment is usually required – with any necessary backup materials and support – so that the exercise can be actually achieved.

So, when planning for a practical, the champion will be considering the equipment which will be necessary – and the conditions under which the learner can learn to operate it. There are many occasions when you can't use the live situation.

- Equipment may be moving too quickly to accommodate the slower learning process (as with any production belt process).
- Activities might inadvertently feed dummy training examples into the live computer system, bringing confusion to the (contact centre) operation.
- Direct learner exposure to fully working equipment might be too dangerous, under Health and Safety rulings.

Selecting the correct level

As champion, you must consider these possible eventualities and select the correct level of practical involvement relative to your learner's current competency. Having established the practicalities and probable outcome of the session, you'll then be able to identify the equipment and other resources you'll require.

Because it's likely that the learning event will be taking place in your, and the learner's, own department, most of the equipment should be fairly readily available. However, this is where the decisions regarding actual methods of using equipment in learning mode will be very important. Sometimes, the standard set-up or on-line system won't be appropriate for learning purposes, so you should clarify these operational decisions before finally sourcing the necessary kit and arrangements. In your earlier stages of championing, you might benefit from the advice of others on this.

Lack of preparation

An ill-prepared champion (not you of course!) trying to organise facilities at the last moment before a planned championing event, may have to "make do" with what's available and easily possible. Even worse, some might finish up distorting the learning to suit the equipment availability – in effect changing the learning outcome. This is just bad planning and organisation, with the result that standards begin to slip. This might escalate to the point where the individual learner could ask the champion to discuss these shortfalls, with reference to the championing agreement.

So, even if you – as champion – can easily lay hands on the necessary equipment within your department, you may still require some assistance and advice from the support function in order to create the correct learning experience. The training department especially should be able to help you select the best techniques to apply – and make suggestions regarding appropriate practical exercises.

Development support function (DSF)

The development support function (DSF), incorporating HR, training and senior management, has a broad and very necessary role to play in encouraging and growing this integrated development. The proposed new role may be a different angle on their traditionally understood range of responsibilities – so it may take some time and a lot of discussion, before they fit comfortably into the integrated system.

The revised DSF role is:

- emphasising a more supportive stance;
- offering guidance;
- arranging resource provision;
- supporting time allocations and staff release; and
- suggesting workplace learning techniques rather than the assumed provision of more formal training responsed.

There is, of course, still an important place for training department provision of formal training courses, especially where several people need to learn the same information at the same time. But complementing this, the ever-growing body of workplace champions has got to be seen as a fantastic additional asset, responding to specific development needs at individual level.

Perhaps one of the most important attitude changes required by DSF members is that they can accept and support champions as part-time, one-to-one, workplace coaches and mentors, who can bring a wealth of experience and potential to the realm of staff development. Their roles should be reinforced and never taken for granted by the DSF (or the company generally). It's the joint responsibility of both workplace champions (individually or as some form of collective) and the DSF to agree ground rules and timescales for co-operation. This has got to be supported by senior management, both dynamically and consistently.

Nurturing co-operation

Let's play "devil's advocate" for a moment. It's evidently very important that a strong rapport is allowed to develop between workplace champions and DSF members. This will require all-round effort and understanding from all participants.

You might understandably feel that you'll only get involved in workplace championing if the DSF will "pull its weight" and provide the support you require, when you require it. However, the DSF might equally feel that some of their traditional control has been removed. Additionally, they might believe that the large-scale involvement of people as (what they might perceive to be) amateur trainers, is not necessarily an overall benefit. There almost certainly will be a range of pre-conceptions to deal with.

Consistent co-operation

It does therefore become a mutual, confidence-building exercise. You, as champion, have to prove that you can work with individual learners and develop their understanding and competency levels. The support functions have to show that they can give assistance as required – and can encourage a wide range of workplace champions to become more proficient. As a new workplace champion, work quietly with the Training Department/HR – don't even refer to them as the Development Support Function until they do so themselves. Give them as much notice as possible and ask their advice rather than telling them what it is that you need from them. When you do make requests, do all this on a professional level of giving and receiving equally. You are the subject expert.

It's just common sense and basic interpersonal skills, really. The atmosphere of co-operation, once gained and maintained, is well worth the effort.

The final plan

So – where are we along the development track?

We've –

- got our learner prepared for his development event;
- established specifically what his championing need is;
- planned the progression of "bite-sized chunks";
- arranged for the equipment or other supporting resources;
- made arrangements for the correct learning environment;
- liaised with the DSF to get any required support/information; and
- organised schedules to free up both yourself and the learner.

What else might we need, before starting our actual development event?

Requirements will differ with specific subjects, of course, as well as a range of other variables. It will help if you can think about some specific event which you might be involved in championing in the future. Try to identify particular requirements which may be "add-on extra" requirements for that particular event.

The following check list may help –

Action Time 9.1

Checklist for particular session plan

- *Particular learner (or starter learning level).*
- *Particular subject area.*
- *Key expected goal(s) or outcome(s).*
- *Technique(s) you might apply.*
- *Equipment/resources you might need.*
- *Sequence of learning "chunks".*
- *Methods of reinforcing each "chunk".*
- *Method of checking outcome achievement.*
- *Any other requirements.*

So, now we're progressing

You should:

- Feel fairly confident about your first session, if you've been wise and selected a reasonably easy, controllable subject.
- Have identified an enthusiastic individual learner, to allow you to concentrate on content and competence, rather than convincing him/her.
- Have given the event enough thought to be clear in your mind about your sequence of "learning chunks" and the required final outcome.
- Be aware of the key support resources necessary for effective championing.

If you have these foundations right, you should feel quietly confident, if slightly apprehensive. Incidentally, feeling slightly nervous before a championing session is OK. It means you're thinking about what you're doing, concerned as to how the individual learner is going to respond and consciously focusing on the steps and stages you have to cover. Experiencing a slight nervous tension can be motivating.

Defining your session

Think of your championing session as –

- a conversation based upon a structure;
- a chance to demonstrate some of the finer skills which you've learned through experience;
- the experience of helping a colleague to develop a new skill and competence; and
- an opportunity to make sure that your workplace colleague will apply the standards and procedures you consider to be important.

It could be an enjoyable experience for all concerned!

Getting your learning environment right

Working environments will vary – you may be working in an open plan area, with all the noise and distraction problems which that can create.

You may be able to find a quiet place in which you can both shut yourselves away, to assist focus. It's really important to remove distractions and interruptions – thirty minutes of undisturbed workplace championing will be much more effective than an hour disturbed by intermittent phone calls or heads popped round the door for "just a quick query". If everyone is really supporting the growth of a workplace development strategy – they have to demonstrate this support by their actions and not just make appropriate comments when it suits.

With these ground rules in place, don't be afraid to have a sign up saying "Do not disturb for the next half hour". Get your ground rules established and stick to them, however senior the head which is appearing round the doorpost!

Right – you know your own working environment better than anyone, so spend a moment reviewing the development environment you can expect. You can use the following checklist as a prompt – but think outside the box to come up with additional aspects relevant to your particular situation. Use that right brain!

Focus Time 9.2

Workplace Championing Location – Checklist

- *Specific location*
- *Any distraction problems? Y/N If yes, how to deal with them?*
- *Basic facilities required (for an identified event)*
- *Supporting resources required*
- *Equipment required*
- *Method of use – on-line/off-line/specific learning mode*
- *Methods of time control to be applied*
- *Methods of controlling privacy/disruption etc*
- *Reinforcement exercises planned*
- *Any further considerations*

The purpose of using this type of checklist approach is to take the pressure off trying to remember everything immediately prior to the learning session. You'll have enough to concentrate on when applying the actual session content and championing techniques – make it easier for yourself by planning the environment beforehand.

Asking questions

Using questions to progress the discussion is a very good technique to apply in our informal championing. There are several different ways of using questions. They keep you focusing on the individual learner and his/her level of knowledge and him/her actively concentrate on the subject and its application. Active questioning also encourages the sub-division of the learning into the bite-sized chunks that we've established as being important.

Listen to the answers – and ask supplementary questions to probe deeper.

Open and closed questions

The idea is that open questions (how, why, what, when, where) encourage discussion while closed questions seek a yes/no type response. There is scope for using both. The open question encourages elaboration while the closed question clarifies the stance. You might thus use the technique of asking the closed question to establish "Yes" or "No", followed by a series of open questions to confirm knowledge of detail.

Case example

So, you might have a conversation along the lines of:
"Do you know the names of the various control functions here?"
"Yes – well most of them."
"Which ones don't you know?"
"This knob here ... and that switch there ... and the main output."
"OK – let's focus on them. What do you think this switch controls?"
Notice, you don't necessarily get a brief response when you ask a closed question. Think of a closed question such as:
"Did you go somewhere nice for your holidays last summer?"
The answer is likely to go beyond the "Yes" or "No" and provide in-depth detail of the holiday experience, with no further prompting from the questioner.

Phatic communion

This is another type of question where the questioner repeats what the person has just said, in order to encourage him/her to say more. It's a technique where the questioner doesn't therefore add much to the discussion. Constructively – you can use this if you're trying to get the learner to expand his/her real thoughts and views, where your open questions might influence the responses.

Case example

So, you could have a conversation along the lines of:
"I've already tried this technique two or three times."
"So, you've already used it?"
"Yes, it worked very well when I'd calibrated the equipment properly beforehand."
"So, you'd say calibration was important then?"

Keeping focus on the outcome

We've spoken a lot about the importance of preparation. This ensures that you're clear about the –

- sequence you'll be following during the session; and
- activities and exercises which will be involved.

You should have given some thought to the methods you'll use to check the learner's understanding. Use open rather than closed questions to probe detail. If you have problems spontaneously formulating clear questions, prepare a few before the session. This will help you come over more positively – and improve your confidence.

Written sequence plans

Having some form of plan of the key areas you intend to cover – and the likely sequence – is a good idea. Working one-to-one, you want to be in the situation where you can be flexible, expanding and contracting detail and information to meet the individual's real needs. But you do want to have a reference point, to ensure that you can return to progressing through the session as intended.

Brief session plans

In education, these are referred to as "lesson plans" and become an important element of teaching assessments. Workplace championing does not require this full level of formality so, in your case, the session plan could literally be as brief as notes on the back of the proverbial envelope. Because you're dealing with a subject about which you're very familiar, the content shouldn't be a problem. The important elements are –

- knowing the key information which must be imparted;
- being aware of the logical sequence of presenting the detail, where relevant;
- having a means of checking that you're progressing as intended; and
- stating the intended objective and identifying how to check its achievement.

Having this type of checklist will give you added confidence – and will make sure that you cover all the key points you've planned to include. Suitably filed, it becomes a useful reference resource when you're required to do a similar exercise with another individual learner in the future. This will ensure the consistency of your message – while allowing your creativity to respond flexibly as required with your next learner.

Perhaps a good championing session can be summed up by remembering the alphabet sequence: P, Q, R, S – standing for:

- PLAN
- QUESTION
- REINFORCE
- SEQUENCE

Communication and Rapport

Earlier, we were describing the holistic effect as "an outcome which is worth more than the sum of its parts". Developing a positive rapport through good workplace championing is a living example of this holistic effect.

Taken in slightly simplistic terms –

Before a championing event

- We have a champion who knows "X" and an individual learner who doesn't, where "X" is represented by the session objectives or outcomes.

After the event

- We have an individual learner who is now informed about "X"

But also –

- A champion who is better informed about getting the detail across.
- A deeper understanding existing between champion and individual learner.

It's also probable that a better general working relationship will result between the two, producing add-on benefits to the effective operation of the department.

And so the holistic effect develops.

Your current interest in involvement in workplace championing may be because you're already a positive communicator and active team member. Your effectiveness will continue to grow as you monitor and build upon the workplace championing effects. As this overall championing involvement grows, team synergy will evolve naturally within your department – and across departments, once the overall strategy has broken through any barriers that may currently exist.

The learning development session

One of the key priorities for effective workplace championing is that we're confident about –

- the basic structure;
- the planned progress; and
- the intended outcome

– of our session.

Remember, we're not overly concerned about methods of professional delivery, the use of complex resources and the other criteria for more formal learning presentation. Our key delivery goals for champions is that they are competent at relating to the learner, communicating at his/her required level, as well as being able to establish that his/her objectives have been met.

Let's think through the steps and stages of an actual development session.

Action Time 9.3

Picture the desk where our hypothetical knowledge championing session is taking place. Thanks to detailed planning, we've managed to provide all the resources which we've decided are necessary, set the room up to meet our requirements and provided the equipment which is necessary to get the message across.

Here are some of the items on our session preparation checklist:

- checklist of sequence of learning points to cover during session;
- reference books and materials (with particular items tabbed for access);
- any specifically prepared illustrations, handouts etc;
- any equipment or models to be used as reference visual aids;
- paper and pens for note-taking and point-illustration during session; and
- comfortable chairs and table in a quiet area.

You may be able to think of some extra ones, which might be valid and necessary for the particular types of development you may apply in your workplace.

Action Time 9.4

Try this short exercise.

Decide on a subject area for which you might be asked to act as a workplace champion. Think small and specific – select a particular, finite activity.

Under the various bullet point headings above, identify some of the specifics which you might require, alongside my parallel example.

Subject: *Designing a website*
Checklist: *Identify page range/design home page/*
establish control parameters etc
Reference: *"Frontpage in Easy Steps" etc*
Materials: *Copies of existing website pages*
Examples of copy text for page(s)
Handout: *Definitions and key operations*
Equipment: *Access to internet computer*
Planned follow-up consolidation: Design of specific pages

You'll see that, if you're knowledgeable about your subject (which you are), there's not a lot of preparation required. It's largely noting down the:

- *particular outcome or objective you're aiming to achieve;*
- *key areas that you'll cover;*
- *sequence that these will take;*
- *stages where consolidation will be necessary;*
- *resources and equipment which are required;*
- *final consolidation of the new learning; and*
- *possible follow-up wor kplace reinforcement of the new learning.*

With your various plans, props and procedures around you in this way, you're ready for action as a workplace champion.

10 The New Workplace Champion – Checklist for Review Stage

One-minute overview

This chapter starts with a review of competency levels and progress – and considerations regarding specialisation. It lists and explores a range of championing criteria, with a range of tips and techniques for effective championing. The areas of building rapport and professional relationships are examined, as well as working with development support. Techniques for working pro-actively with individual learners, and responding to particular learning priorities, are reviewed. Several case studies are used to illustrate different levels and techniques. The chapter ends by reviewing how champions can self-assess their own progress and identify areas for further development.

One of the good things about thinking objectively and having a clear idea of your goals and outcomes is that you know when you've arrived at your destination. Remember our visualisation of the development track. If you've taken note of the journey along the way (and the milestones which you've been passing en-route), you should be clear about how competent you are at the various skills you've experienced during your progression – and any outstanding matters remaining.

Competency at individual level

Regular practice and experience is necessary to reinforce learning, before any learner can become fully competent and up to speed. Any given learner will be more competent at some tasks than others. This will reflect on the amount of extra experience (and potentially, remedial inputs) that the individual learner must have to consolidate the learning. Considering the situation honestly and objectively, any individual's competency levels will fluctuate. We must accept that many people will continue to have some "blind spots" – learning areas which they find exceptionally difficult or skills or knowledge areas which they will never be naturally skilful at achieving, however hard they try.

Part of holistic self analysis is to be able to highlight these blind spots within our overall analysis of strengths and shortfall areas. You may have a real shortfall area that, however hard you try, you know that you'll never be totally proficient at performing. In the current atmosphere of specialisation, it may be possible to trade non-involvement in this with greater involvement in one or some of your real strength areas. This is how specialists evolve.

So, there's no failure in acknowledging that you're better at some skills than others and specialising, rather than necessarily becoming an "all-rounder". Individual continuing professional development then concentrates on keeping up-to-speed with directly related skills and techniques. Remember, if your strengths are restricted but specialised, you've got to follow the motto – "don't be good, be brilliant".

Know thyself – some more

Each of us will be knowledgeable about particular subject areas, skills and activities that we would feel comfortable imparting to others – so these are the ones that we should propose as our "menu" for possible championing involvement.

Similarly, each of us might have preferred ways of passing this information to someone else.

You might –

- Be happier demonstrating the operation of a piece of kit, rather than sitting down trying to explain the theory and legislation behind some particular job aspect.
- Feel confident working one-to-one but feel scared at the thought of working with a small group.
- Be comfortable running a single, one-off session covering a particular "chunk" of learning – but have mental overload at the thought of planning and running a sequence of sessions in an extended development programme.

As your confidence grows, you may even feel that you can offer championing help in areas where you are perhaps not the total expert. Although less than ideal, it's better for the company that a subject is covered by a workplace champion doing his/her best, following considered policies and processes. The alternative is a situation where there are individuals who cannot proceed productively until some form of future training is arranged for them.

Life is a learning experience: review and evaluate your skills

In order to widen our potential range, we should consider ways of reviewing and evaluating our own championing skills, in order to monitor our own competency levels. If we're expecting our individual learners to review their performance and any potential blocks as they progress, we should be open to doing the same for our own performance.

Focus Time 10.1

Imagine the scene – you've just finished running (or delivering) a workplace championing session. The individual learner has left the room and you're sitting alone having a few moments of reflection.

Reflective learning should be another skill in your tool kit. It basically encourages you to pause and spend a little time reviewing –

- *what has been experienced between champion and learner;*
- *how and when it can be applied; and*
- *what additional activities might be necessary to reinforce the learning further.*

So, you're thinking about how the session has gone, what the high and low points were – and how you might do it slightly differently for that individual learner, given another opportunity.

What criteria or standards would you use to make your judgements?
They might follow headings such as:

- *completeness of planning;*
- *interruptions – and how handled;*
- *rapport between champion and learner;*
- *correctness of level of materials re your learner;*
- *relevance of materials and session to learner's needs;*
- *progressive flow and precision of session;*
- *acceptability of learning room/environment;*
- *flexibility of session to meet learner needs;*
- *relationship of session to additional learner development needs; and*
- *overall feeling about my effectiveness as a champion on this session.*

Some of these have already been considered during the earlier planning stages. We can now compare the reality of the completed session with the previous planning, to see how the two have married together.

Of course, always bear in mind that proper one-to-one training will vary from session to session (or more importantly, individual to individual). This can leave you with the situation where techniques, stances and priorities which work wonderfully well for one learner may be inappropriate for another. So, don't totally select or reject some technique or resource for one learner based on its level of success with another.

The better response is to have a few alternative strategies available – with the resources available to allow them to happen. Then, if the session is beginning to go wrong because of some mismatch between particular learner and method, you can pull back and try a fresh approach.

Detailed planning

There are various questions you can ask yourself:

- Did the session progress as you had planned it to progress?
- Did you break the flow to find additional resources or equipment?
- Was the learning level as you expected/were you able to adjust?
- Were you able to cover the detail you planned in the time allocated?
- Was the starting level appropriate? Did you have to review basics?

Because you're normally working with a single learner, you should be aware of his/her level – and plan accordingly. Awareness of the individual and expected levels should then give you spin-off indicators of the range of supporting resources and environment you'll require. Normally, deficiencies in planning shouldn't be a problem ... there's little excuse, really, if you know the individual learner.

Interruptions – and how to combat them

This will depend, to some extent, on the environment that you've set up – and how used you and other staff are to working in that environment. If someone is used to working in enclosed offices with limited distractions, busy open plan office environments can be difficult for creative work. Where staff-members are used to the open plan environment, distractions are accommodated relatively easily. Once again, it's a case of being aware of the learner's views as well as your own.

To really combat interruptions, a meeting room with closed door and an engaged sign outside is the ultimate solution. Unplug any internal phones and, if anyone should interrupt – despite the sign – tell them firmly that you'll get back to them within the hour (assuming that the normal championing session is that or less). Then, champion and learner can get down to business.

Where both parties are used to open plan working environments, background noise and activity may not be a distraction. For interruption-free working in this environment, the company or department should have a policy for flagging up the need to be left to concentrate. Caps, ear protectors, flags and signs can all be used to signify "Do not disturb" – the symbol doesn't really matter as long as the message is respected by everyone.

If there are no official ground rules, set your own. Once set, don't be afraid to be emphatic about reinforcing them. It'll improve the effectiveness of the championing.

Rapport between champion and individual learner

In any review, you should consider how the rapport developed between yourself and your individual learner. This is very important in one-to-one development, in order that two-way communication can be allowed to flourish.

What are some of the key indicators you might be looking out for?

They might include:

- How freely were the conversations flowing?
- Was the learner volunteering questions and information?
- How confident was s/he to try out the new skills etc discussed?
- How relaxed were you – do you recall any humorous moments?
- If you experienced any blocks – how easily did you overcome them?
- Did you discuss any possible ideas for workplace reinforcement?

In building a rapport, you're trying to develop the atmosphere where you can work together as equals. The relationship will be influenced slightly by the normal management style within your organisation – although, if you are a manager, you could choose to be friendlier and more personable when a champion than you might be normally when managing the same individual.

Professional relationships: retaining standards

Although developing a friendly atmosphere, you should still retain a degree of professionalism. The ground rules for this are set in the organisation and inter-relationship established for the session.

Professionalism standards might include –

- never discuss colleagues at a personal level, "behind their backs";
- use proper names and official titles – not nicknames etc;

- focus on the work in hand and don't digress into private conversation;
- follow company procedures and processes, without open criticism; and
- maintain a professional distance when testing or checking on progress.

Focus Time 10.2

If you review the Presentation Planning Meeting (final) section in the Case Study in chapter seven, you should spot various instances of this professionalism being maintained as the group members interacted holistically. With reference to the criteria set out in the bullet points above, you may find it useful to try to identify a few illustrative examples.

Levels of rapport

It's quite normal to develop different levels of rapport with different individual learners, dependent on a whole range of characteristics (such as age, social and intellectual standing, experience, beliefs, interests etc). You select your personal friends applying the same types of criteria. However, it's important to remember that, in championing, you're developing a positive working relationship rather than a close personal friendship. It's usually preferable to maintain some degree of professional reserve.

Appropriate materials

From your own experience of using materials as a student or learner, you'll know that some materials will appear too complex for you to understand comfortably, while others are over-simplistic. It'll be the same for your individual learner. Progressively, as you get to know him/her better, you should be able to identify expected levels of prior knowledge. You'll then be in a better position to make judgements about foundation levels of knowledge and understanding, as well as strengths and shortfalls.

In the earlier stages of working with a new learner, you'll have to test out these levels gently. Adult learners, especially working one-to-one with you, will be trying hard to understand. It's therefore safer to assume that, if there is a breakdown in understanding, it's more likely to be your explanation or illustration which requires improving than the learner's attention. Think positively and openly.

This resource selection is an area where you might benefit from some help and advice from the DSF. They should be able to advise you of sources for accessing learning resources and how to select the most appropriate, relative to learner levels and styles. Professionally designed resources should come with stated objectives or outcomes attached – be wary of those which don't, or use vague statements along the "show a better understanding of ...." variety. These statements mean very little in real, measurable terms.

You can always set up a little test for yourself.

Action Time 10.1

The next time you're using what you consider to be a good reference resource, illustration, handout, textbook or whatever, try to identify what makes it "good" in your eyes. Of course your personal criteria are just that, so your preferences may not be those of others but it will at least give you some indicators to check out when selecting materials for your championing sessions.

Build up a checklist of the criteria which are important to you, adding to the following:

- *colour versus black and white;*
- *use of bullet point statements;*
- *photographs versus line drawings;*
- *use of plain English; and*
- *appropriate amount of detail.*

Materials and session appropriate to needs

This is an extension to – and refinement of – the previous section. It also links with your awareness of the sequencing of the learning, its subdivision into those "bite-sized chunks" and the knowledge of how the individual learner will be applying the new information directly in the workplace. This is the practical reinforcement which comes after the championing input.

Judging appropriateness is probably one of the most "scientific" of the assessments you'll have to make – and might be an area which you in turn could require some training in order to achieve it correctly. If a work-specific learning objective has been stated clearly, it should be possible to assess the degree to which it's been met.

Focus on the learner

In objective statements, you're focusing on the learner when you're establishing levels – and on the real workplace practicalities when you're considering appropriate applications. It's not what works for you – it's what works for the individual learner. If you discover that it doesn't work, it's up to you to adapt your approach until it does. The onus is on you to provide the message in the most appropriate way to meet the needs of your particular individual learner. This is the secret of success!

Try to monitor the effectiveness of your message *during* the session and attempt to make any refinements to improve its effectiveness as the session progresses. This pro-active approach is more valuable than reviewing mistakes after the event is completed. It's really too late to then come up with alternative solutions which might have worked better.

Because you're responding to the needs of a single, identified learner, there's no excuse for not targeting that individual clearly and correctly. Also, if your level of rapport allows you to relate to him/her during the session, you should be able to make any adjustments necessary as you progress, to maintain progress.

Adjusting to individual development

Any assessed conclusions concerning the learner's skills, competency levels and levels of concentration would have to be fed back into the system. This will ensure that the subsequent championing sessions and the necessary workplace reinforcement can be revised accurately to meet each individual learner's needs and levels as precisely as possible. Keeping an open, flexible mind is thus very important. Using "off-the-shelf" training generally can cause problems because its effectiveness will vary between learners and preferred learning styles. Don't fall into the trap of using the same techniques and styles unthinkingly for different learners. This is moving back into the "one size fits all" form of training, which we've already rejected.

We would expect the programme content to be much the same if not identical. The variety in delivery will evolve more from the levels, previous experience and competencies, as well as the preferred learning styles of the different individual learners. Never forget the benefits of wide-ranging individuality – it's what gives your holistic team the bonus of combined skills and applications, when the synergy begins to activate.

Progressive flow and precision

This is a check on whether you've got your objectives right – in the shape of your building bricks of knowledge, understanding and application (or detail, explanation and real practice). It's also the opportunity to assess your ability to set and achieve clear targets or outcomes.

Remember, also, when you're thinking in those "bite-sized chunks" that the knowledge/understanding/application progress can recycle regularly during the championing event. This allows you and the learner to consolidate the learning at each stage – thus giving a greater probability that the new learning is being cemented firmly in place.

Focus Time 10.3

Think, first of all about a championing session which could use one, full-scale sequence of the three stages.

In an earlier chapter, we considered the activity involved in learning how to plan out a business report. This would involve:

KNOWLEDGE:	*The structural headings of the report; definitions and explanations of key words; use of appendices and summaries.*
UNDERSTANDING:	*The relationship of the different report sections; the choice of detail levels to be included; purpose of the range of reports; range of styles of writing applied to different reports.*
APPLICATION:	*Selection of type and style of report to meet business need; writing structural plan and sample sections for selected report; identification and drafting of related appendices.*

Working through these stages would give you a complete development session, with the outcome that by the end, the learner would be competent to:

structure and draft a business report, following approved layout plans and including all required elements, to present and support the results of a particular business research exercise.

Now, let's think about a longer, slightly more complex development exercise. As a totally different experience, let's consider the preparatory stages before shearing sheep.

There are various stages in the learning progress here. There's:

- *setting up and running the mechanical shearing equipment;*
- *the handling of the sheep to create immobility;*

- *the technique of shearing; and*
- *the sequence of shearing, to give a single fleece of wool.*

Which of these would you consider to be the hardest to become confidently competent at achieving?

Yes – probably the practical stages of actually shearing the sheep ... with the manhandling of the sheep over onto its rump and positioning to make it immobile coming a close second. The other two (knowing the machinery and the theory behind the shearing sequence) are both fairly theoretical, so have less fear factor of things going wrong. There are of course the additional practical elements of equipment maintenance.

Sheep management

Taking the two activities directly involving in handling the animal, we have first of all the act of immobilising the sheep ready for shearing. We would deliver this by:

- *first explaining the theory of turning the sheep onto its back (knowledge);*
- *then, demonstrating the practicalities, using a sheep (understanding); and*
- *thirdly, getting the learner to try – with guidance (application).*

The final practical stage here involves standing the sheep on its rump and immobilising it by turning its head to one side. (Leaning back against the handler's legs, with one leg bent back, a sheep will tend to stay perfectly still in this position without struggling.)

At this stage, the individual learner has gone through and basically practised the key handling stage. In other words, s/he has demonstrated that s/he can handle a sheep – but we need not necessarily be confident that s/he can hold the sheep correctly when concentrating on shearing. As it's very easy to nick or cut the sheep if it moves while shearing is in progress, we need to be sure of the learner's animal-handling competency before s/he progresses towards learning how to shear the sheep.

Confident handling

As a final practice, therefore, we'd get the individual learner to move a sheep to various positions, following our requests, so that it is held immobile lying on one side, then rolled over on its back to lie on its other side – and held leaning back on its rump. We might then extend this further by getting the learner to run the cutter over the beast as if to shear it – but with the power switched off. This would further reinforce the need to stabilise the sheep with one hand, while cutting with the other.

Mechanical Shearing

As you can imagine, learning the practical shearing process (having gone through the theory, step by step) must be done in an extended sequence of hands-on steps. This is covered in shepherding textbooks – or by attending Wool Board courses – if you secretly want to downshift and have a flock of sheep!

Conclusion

The important point here is that you have to see the learning in steps and stages – and consolidate each stage to an acceptable level before progressing further. This gives the flow and sequence, while ensuring that each stage has been first achieved to an acceptable level of competency. The additional workplace reinforcement and practice that we can virtually guarantee through workplace championing is a very valuable bonus.

The learning space and environment

This is where you're asking yourself questions such as – how was it for you? – and your individual learner? Was it noisy, cramped ... uncomfortable? Were there too many interruptions? Did you have all the equipment you needed – and did it all function as it should?

You certainly should be able to analyse in hindsight what was good and bad about the overall learning environment. The idea is that, through experience, you'll gradually learn to spot potential problems before they happen ... and can therefore set up an event so that the learning atmosphere is just as you would choose it to be.

The environment will of course vary depending on the type of learning; the practical nature of the subject; the normal working conditions within your company ... all these types of things. Some individual learners (and champions as well) are affected by the environment more than others. If known, this should be taken into account when planning. For example, you might spend time trying to find a quiet room, where this may not be an issue for the learner. In this instance, you might have been better channelling your efforts into considering the session content in greater detail.

Meeting individual learner needs

We are likely to know the individual learner for each of our workplace championing events. Through a developed rapport, we should be able to plan the session to meet his/her needs. If we've got the level right, the session should progress smoothly.

Life tends not to flow quite so uneventfully, however – so we may certainly experience operational or content upsets during the actual event. This is where a flexible approach to learning is valuable, allowing you to step back slightly from the planned path and apply alternative ways to successfully reach the next milestone.

Order out of apparent chaos: strategies and solutions to problems

Remember the spaghetti-like jumble of individual paths along our developmental track?

- Some of the visible detours on any selected path will have been caused by the individual learner seeking a way round a particular obstacle or block.
- Some reactions might be almost instantaneous – other detours may delay matters while the individual identified an alternative solution.
- Other alternative responses may have been suggested or initiated by the champion, rapidly judging the situation and spotting alternative strategies.

Given time and experience, you'll be able to pre-consider a range of potential responses to given situations. Thinking about this before the event allows you to be ready to select an alternative way forward, when the block happens. You are then in a better position to negotiate your way confidently round any milestone obstacle the instant it gets in your way.

Effective control and progress is rarely down to luck – it's more likely to be due to objective thinking, strategic planning and a flexible, open approach.

Seeing the overall picture: awareness of additional related development areas

On occasions where particular individual development sessions link with additional learning needs for that learner, you (as workplace champion) need to step back if you can, in order to see the bigger picture. Where the overall needs of that individual learner may be serviced by a range of different champions, a higher level of co-ordination through the development support function will also be valuable.

When reviewing the success of a particular learning session, you (as champion) should be aware of additional related development areas, either that the learner has already achieved – or that s/he has still to study.

Examples

Let's say that you were championing someone on effective meetings communication – focusing on minutes writing. If you knew that this individual learner was already competent at report writing (perhaps due to an earlier learning session), you could cross-refer to details of structure, grammar and levels of formality of expression which s/he would already know.

Equally, when championing a particular subject, key problems and blind spots could be identified which might need supplementary development inputs, perhaps under a different subject heading. These might already be planned as part of another development session, increasing its priority to be completed.

This overviewing helps champions to order the learning relationships and prioritise the responses flexibly. It also assists in the overall co-ordination of workplace championing sessions and individual development programmes, through the DSF.

Relating to other development needs of the learner

As well as the important information spin-off between different development events for any single learner, there will also be a synergy or holistic benefit from sharing learning outcomes between various individual learners. We've already discussed the holistic benefits achieved when individual competencies combine. If you recall the final group presentation in the chapter seven case study, the act of combining the varied individual key skills created an overall group presentation. The whole dynamic was worth more than the sum of the individual inputs.

How different learning events and learner competencies can combine

As the range and volume of individual workplace championing activities expand within your department or company, you'll see how different learning events and learner competencies can combine. At a simple level, you could use one learner (who has recently become competent at some activity) to monitor another newer learner who may be tentatively carrying out his first workplace reinforcement exercise. Both are having their learning reinforced in slightly different ways.

Shared experiences and applications

At a more complex level, you can combine individuals who are being coached and mentored in different but related skills, to allow them to share experiences and applications. This atmosphere of mutual assistance is one of the benefits of a workplace championing atmosphere, once it has been established. It happens on the sports field, in industrial units and in business departments. Where in existence, colleagues were willingly giving their time to share experiences with others, in order to help them progress. On many occasions, it only required a brief remedial input to unlock a learner who had become "stuck" when attempting a new procedure, allowing him/her to become operational once more. That's effective and responsive development for you! That's the holistic effect.

Seeking opportunities

The more that you, as a champion, are aware of the full range of coaching, mentoring and other informal activities being practised or planned, the more you'll be able to respond to and apply the different skills, needs and competency levels, to enhance the overall workplace effectiveness.

Keep your eye on the bigger picture – it's the holistic way.

How effective was I as a workplace champion in this session?

There's the real question to ask yourself. How do you gauge your effectiveness? There are various checklists we've developed throughout this book, identifying the range of criteria which make a "good workplace champion". Check some of these again, to help you judge your effectiveness:

- Chapter 1 : Championing – Key Skills — Page [6]
- Chapter 3 : Key skills and competencies — Page [23]
- Chapter 3 : Workspace development priorities — Page [41]
- Chapter 5 : Championing skills — Page [55-56]
- Chapter 5 : Consistency and holistic thinking — Page [70]
- Chapter 6 : Key requirements — Page [74-75]
- Chapter 6 : Competency checklist — Page [79]
- Chapter 6 : Initial activities — Page [81]
- Chapter 6 : Preparing Champion teams — Page [84]
- Chapter 8 : Know thyself — Page [103]
- Chapter 8 : Championing hierarchy — Page [105]
- Chapter 9 : Championing agreement — Page [116]
- Chapter 10: Evaluation criteria — Page [129]

Lots of checklists to refer to once more – this may be recapping but ... it will help to cement the different ideas, criteria, outcomes and standards you're trying to achieve.

Now that you're better informed about your priorities, you may find it beneficial to make some notes of any future key actions.

Personal motivation

You, more than anyone, should be aware of your strengths and shortfalls, if you're honest with yourself. You'll know the aspects of championing which you (perhaps secretly) find rather difficult ... and therefore feel good within yourself when things go right during a session. You'll be aware of the techniques which you've been quietly trying to master ... and you'll know the buzz you get when you finally feel that you're coping with it successfully. And – if your learner is activated and gives you some indications that your championing session has worked well for him or her – well, that's a real added bonus!

Well done!

11 The Holistic Way

One-minute overview

This chapter reviews the meaning and applications of holistic thinking within a business context, responding to changes in society and its effects. We consider the applications of the holist movement and synergy in group development, comparing these with sporting applications. Within the combination of consistency and time allocation, we review techniques for building positive, conducive atmospheres, with reference to stated holistic tenets. The chapter considers the applications of work/life balance from a holistic viewpoint, through a range of examples and underlines the importance of "big picture" thinking. It underscores the overall attitudes which will improve co-operative outcomes, through retaining an open and flexible mind and continually attempting to develop and improve.

We've been referring to "the holistic way" periodically throughout this book, defining holistic as "creating a whole which is greater than the sum of its parts, by ordered grouping". You've probably already come across the expression used in relation to healthy living, where applying a wider range of potential responses will result in a greater gain than focusing on one particular area. In our Case Study in chapter seven, we experienced a team, working to develop a group presentation, which applied a breadth of expertise that no one team member could provide on his/her own. This was a clear illustration of holistic thinking applied within a business context, with the group result more dynamic than any one individual's performance.

Holistic Business

Generally, we're becoming a world of individual thinkers. Internet consciousness has encouraged us to discover product detail and availability for ourselves, accessing keen prices and specialist opportunities. The wider accessibility of information has allowed us to probe and question, making us more aware of the implications of decisions being made in our name. Companies too think in a more individual way, embracing such things as outsourcing, short-term contracts and interim management. These are – or should be – all applying focused rather than selfish criteria, potentially amalgamating the individual needs of both employee and business.

The alternative way: balance and being positive

Through these considerations, people are becoming increasingly conscious of the possibility of and potential ... even need ... for an alternative way. As they think more individually –

- opportunities for extreme advancement may be turned down in favour of "spending more time with the family";
- increasing numbers of people are considering downshifting as a means of gaining greater control of their present and future work/life balance; and

- some companies are beginning to realise that creating a positive, stress-reduced working atmosphere will deliver gains overall.

Holist movement

Phrases such as Diversity, Spirituality and Emotional Intelligence are now used without embarrassment, to indicate ways of working which take the needs and priorities of individuals more firmly into consideration. There is also a growing holist movement emphasising the importance of "big picture" awareness and long-term integrated co-operation, within society as well as in business and education.

Several companies – many of them in the ICT and Financial sectors – are creating new work environments which take account of their employees' social, psychological and developmental needs, in the firm belief that an improved ambiance and atmosphere will have a positive effect on quality (not to mention quantity) of work output, through higher job satisfaction.

Progressive development

This is no recent, short-term response – my embryonic integrated triangle concept was originally presented in a paper in 1987 (winning the silver essay award promoted by the then Institute of Training and Development). In the intervening years, various supporting articles have been published in professional journals, advocating co-operative team development and wide-ranging coaching and mentoring strategies within business. Several other consultancies and management colleges also promote the approach, whether or not they overtly refer to it as being holistic.

Holistic team development

It will be valuable for our overall understanding of championing applications if we spend a little time elaborating further on what are considered to be the key holistic criteria and applications.

A prime example – and perhaps the easiest to see in action – is that of combining individual talents within a team to produce an output which is greater than the sum of the individual inputs. This has been illustrated in chapter seven.

Synergy and its positive effects

If you've been involved in working with and developing staff as members of a team – or indeed if you have worked as a member of such a team yourself – you'll be aware of the positive effects of "synergy". Some see this as merely an avoidable example of business jargon. However, many consider that focusing on and striving for a higher level of synergy is worthwhile within a business team, gaining strong motivational effects.

Sports people are vociferous in advocating the benefits of team relationships, with many courses and inspirational presentations based on how they rallied their teams to win. However, this form of sports team motivation can have a fairly limited life time and cycle. Adrenalin-driven team synergy tends to be easier to achieve for a ninety minute football match than in the long-term concentration on goals by all members of a department, as required in business team development.

The key importance of consistency

The importance of consistency is absolutely fundamental. There is nothing worse than working hard to develop a rapport within your departmental team (based on agreed parameters) – only to find that these parameters, or "goalposts", are suddenly moved by the decisions and/or actions of some unthinking manager. Predictably, the result is rapid team de-motivation and a decreasing enthusiasm towards being involved in subsequent projects. The team synergy is immediately damaged.

When setting up a championing strategy, the necessary infrastructure must be first established in-house to guarantee that the overall programme will be both supported and consolidated long-term. Until these foundations are laid and tested, running development sessions for our new workplace champions could be a waste of time.

Agreed and maintained guidelines for the life of the programme

Therefore, an important holistic element necessary for the creation of an atmosphere of team development, is the establishment of these consistent parameters. These will differ between companies, departments and decision-makers – and in some cases may be less-than-perfect. The important thing is that the guidelines are agreed and maintained consistently by all parties over the continuing life of the programme.

This is the reason behind the suggestion that all parties sign up to some form of Workplace Championing agreement (see page [116]). It's also why efforts must be made to build and agree the foundations of the championing initiative prior to final preparatory training for champions.

Making time available for the development sessions

The availability of time off for both champion and individual learner to meet for development sessions is a case in point. If the senior managers involved have agreed that this time will be allowable, then both the champion and learner must feel confident that their arranged sessions will be supported – and continue to be supported. Disruptions such as last minute, unjustified cancellations or either party being called away in mid-session will only act to kill the holistically creative atmosphere ... and demoralise the whole initiative. This consistent approach is crucially important.

Holistic working tenets

In chapter five, we explored some tenets for a holistic way of life (on page [70]), forming the guidelines for a conducive work/life balance. Evidently, the wider the spread of people living and working by these tenets, the more successful the resulting synergy will be. This links with "the hundred monkeys' principle", where a critical mass point is reached, beyond which a particular way of thinking or acting becomes the acceptable norm.

It will be valuable if we reconsider these tenets or principles in slightly greater detail for a moment or two. Some will be more important than others to you – you may even have difficulty in acknowledging one or two of them at this point in your overall holistic development. This is perfectly OK – remember the twisting spaghetti trail!

Action Time 11.1

On page [70], you'll find the list of key tenets towards applying a more holistic way of thinking within a business context. Consider these for a few minutes and relate them to the way you work in your current employment or method of earning a living.

From these ten tenets, select the five which you think are most relevant to the way you would choose to work – and which you consider could be applied in your workplace, either currently or with a bit of foundation building.

It may help you to make a note of these separately.

Now, putting these in the context of how you would ideally choose to work, prioritise these from 1 – 5, with #1 being the most important.

Taking your top two priorities, consider any adjustments which may be necessary to your way of life and work, to allow each to develop positively and openly.

These are your personal "ground rules", which you may have to work to develop.

Short- and longer-term gains

Altruistic, co-operative thinking like this is still seen as being "soft" by some people – and it must be admitted that an individual acting assertively for his/her own ends can often still win in the short-term – the more so if the assertion (or assertiveness) is erring on the side of aggression.

However, if the remainder of the team can continue to work co-operatively, they are in a strong position to emphatically advocate the majority viewpoint, to the stage where it becomes the accepted way forward. It's a mark of the individual's development from assertiveness towards co-operation that s/he can learn to accept the majority view, while perhaps still concentrating some effort on influencing rather than upsetting it. Co-operation is a higher level of business interaction, reaching beyond assertion.

Holistic working atmosphere

This works both ways. It's necessary that the attitudes are present in the key players, so that the atmosphere may develop. It's equally necessary that the atmosphere remains consistent, to permit these holistic attitudes to evolve. This underlines the importance of selecting the first few projects carefully, to encourage both atmosphere and attitudes to grow positively in parallel.

We've been periodically considering the holistic elements which build towards forming a conducive atmosphere. Being realistic, we have to accept that this will evolve at different paces in different organisations. So, any bullet point list of examples may seem normal to some while rather extraordinary to others.

A possible list of adjectives which would describe the atmosphere we're aspiring to create, might include –

- co-operative
- open-minded
- sharing
- communicative
- democratic
- focused

- objective
- motivating
- progressive
- honest

You may find some of these more applicable than others, as they relate to the current status of your working environment. They are, however, all milestones on that intertwining spaghetti trail called "Holistic Development"!

Work/life Balance

This is an area where the critical mass point of popular interest has already been surpassed in the sense that it features in both professional journals and glossy magazines. In holistic terms, it extends beyond the usual focus on working hours and child care, towards a greater concentration on how work and life aspects can interact and affect each other.

Becoming involved

So, for example, we can have an individual who becomes frustrated at work, as his/her established prime business objectives prevent him/her from becoming involved in an area of development personally seen as being very important. Instead of allowing this to affect him/her, s/he could instead become involved in a similar or parallel activity in private life, allowing him/her to practise and develop this particular skill.

Case study example

Earlier, the example was cited where someone perhaps wished to become involved in formal training within his organisation but, because there were no current openings in this area, concentrated instead on improving his public speaking skills in his private life. He could equally become involved in helping with teenager groups – or even doing a bit of sports coaching if his skills permitted.

This enthusiasm for involvement in training could also be channelled into becoming a key workplace champion, of course – or even helping with the initial training and induction of other new champions. There's a range of options open to build and maintain motivation in this example of holistic work/life balance in action.

More work/life balance considerations

There are many instances of this skills transfer between life and work – for example, many mature women who have brought up children successfully through the teenage years become almost natural buddies or champions for young new starts, as they can bring their parenting skills to practical use in the workplace.

So, the balance and sharing of skills and experience is just as important as the allocation of time in work/life balance.

Codes of practise

Another area worthy of consideration is the application of standards, interaction and some form of moral code. There's a strange imbalance in existence where, say, an individual lives by a certain code in his private life (helping and co-operating with others, never pilfering what belongs to someone else, listening patiently as someone tells them a long, rambling story in the pub and so on) but would change dramatically when at work, becoming more self-centred, impatient and wary of hidden agendas. This is more likely to happen when the working environment is both imperfect and inconsistent. Imbalances will exist - but the discrepancies that many people have between work and life mores does bear thinking about.

Focus Time 11.1

Think of any areas within your life and work where you perhaps deal differently with people in these two separate aspects.

For example, perhaps you are less open with people at work; treat the use of office and friends' property differently, or vary your allocation of time for relating and interacting with people.

We're not looking for any instant change here – but rather awareness that perhaps you do have separate work and life egos. If this is the case, give some thought to the reasons for the differences – and consider ways in which you might want to even them out, in order to both live and work in a manner which was closer to your true self.

Other people are experiencing the same complications, of course, which makes it even harder to effect change. Try to separate the areas where you think you can influence change from those where the situation is beyond your control.

This is a difficult concept – but one worth reviewing for a while, to gain a better idea of your personal holistic balance.

If you feel ready, make a note of one or two personal development areas for life and/or work, where you might action yourself to think in a radically different way.

Co-operation and Communication

Many businesses have problems caused by poor communication.

Whether it's –

- someone not taking the time to explain what is required;
- forgetting to advise those involved about schedule or detail changes;
- sharing the wrong information with the wrong people;
- relying on impersonal, "second-hand" forms of communication (such as memo or email) to convey important information;
- people hearing and seeing selectively, or not listening;

- the resultant operational difficulties expand much further than the original communication problem creating them.

We've regularly underlined the importance of champions establishing the correct level of communication to meet the individual learner's level, delivering the information in those "bite-sized chunks" and checking regularly (by listening) to establish that the information has come over clearly enough to be applied constructively.

We've also underlined the benefits of the integrated approach, encouraging any one individual to be both champion and learner for different specific developmental areas – thus remaining aware of the needs and priorities of the one while wearing the hat of the other. (Think about that for a minute!)

Holistic communication

So, looking holistically and being aware of the individual(s) while communicating – by responding to them and adapting the message accordingly – will result in a clearer message and a better end result. Using a variety of media will help the end result as well ... what is it that they say a picture is worth? Techniques and resources must be selected to best meet the needs of the individual learner – giving a holistic learning experience which is more effective than the sum of the individual elements.

Think of the sequence –

- Give the learner a picture to look at and s/he'll learn something from it.
- Detail the key issues to look out for in the picture – and the learner will discover a greater depth of knowledge.
- Get the individual learner to discuss the implications of what s/he is seeing – and the extent of understanding will become greater still.

That's the accumulative holistic effect again .... as well as of course being yet another illustration of the learning objective continuum –

Knowledge – Understanding – Application

Analysing communication effectiveness

Take any communication situation, such as watching television, sitting in a meeting or having a chat with others. When involved in one of these, just for a change, sit back and observe **how** things are being said as well as **what** is being said. Identify what's effective – and how it affects the outcome of the conversation. This is often referred to as "body language" – which in effect goes much deeper (and has a whole body of literature devoted to it) than the usually described hand signals and posture.

- Look out for some of the negatives, such as when people are asking questions but paying next to no attention to the answers they're receiving.
- Listen for particular clichés – and note how they're received.
- Look out for examples of good communication and observe how this builds rapport and reaction.
- Look for positive and negative attitudes being visually flagged subconsciously.
- Look out for individuals who can communicate face-to-face, "on the same wavelength" and watch how this allows the relationship to develop well.
- Establish the types of email that are considered to be "good communication".
- Take time to review and edit any written communication before sending it.

Effective verbal and written communication are key to developing relationships and building rapport – gaining effects which more than justify the time spent considering the best methods and words to be used. Spend that time wisely and enjoy the holistic add-on benefits.

Big Picture thinking – the on-board a helicopter view

OK. Here's another concept that some people dismiss as business-speak jargon. It's basically where you pull back from looking at the particular or minutia and instead overview the broader causes and effects. Think about it for a moment. This is a real arena for projecting holistic conclusions – looking towards the end result, while also considering the individual elements which build towards that final outcome.

Thinking broadly as well as specifically also helps to identify key priorities, as well as particular stances. Generally, this puts you in a stronger position to judge why and when certain activities should be carried out. It also allows you to respond more rapidly when requirements change.

Spotting inter-relationships

Big picture thinking applied in team work helps to –

- establish the inter-relationships between individual members and their different activities;
- identify the key skills required from different individuals – aiding specialisation; and
- indicate why certain things must be done in a certain way to create the most effective end result.

This is where individual assertion can become positively overshadowed by group co-operation, for the overall benefit of the majority.

Getting relationships in focus

Many business and communication problems find their origins in a lack of big picture thinking – where individuals are so caught up in their own particular area of interest that they often neither know nor particularly care about the thoughts and actions of others. In this individually orientated age, this is perhaps to be expected.

The manager as leader

However, where team activities are being encouraged or where individuals are inputting into a larger project, an awareness of inter-relationships and priorities becomes very important. This underlines one of the key roles of the team leader, supervisor or manager – that of keeping an overview of the final requirements and how individual actions must be integrated. This requires the combination within the same person of both good manager (looking inward towards supporting staff effectiveness) and good leader (looking outward entrepreneurially towards the conditions necessary for business to flourish).

Thinking outside the box – blue sky imagination

Thought by some to be pure jargon, this is a perfectly valid goal to aim for – the country would not have its various entrepreneurs to admire if blue sky thinking wasn't an integral part of their management style. Entrepreneurial thinking is even more valuable in the current working environment where parameters become ever-tighter, due to the myriad of directives, procedures, benchmarks, regulations and legislation which appear to emanate from every pore in the business infra-structure.

Championing Example

Thinking holistically outside the box involves combining existing parameters and procedures with identified additional actions, responding to special needs. In championing terms, we might for example have a set procedure which must be learned. This will probably be set down in some form of company standard operational procedure (SOP) document, written by the technical department.

This gives us a first level of "thinking outside the box" – don't use the SOP as your training aid. This is obvious, common sense. However, a common business response to this form of induction training is –

1. Get them to read the SOP.
2. Ask them if they've any questions.
3. Get them to sign off as trained.

It keeps the audit trail complete – which sadly may be the key developmental criterion for such companies. This is not good championing practice.

So, first level thinking outside the box encourages the production of checklists and documents, written in a style that the new learner can understand.

Second level thinking outside the box might then consider the additional tips, techniques and other skills which allow the learner to get more rapidly up to speed performing the new procedure. Notice, we're not suggesting the shortcuts much loved of our experienced "Nellies". We're suggesting additional tips which will make the procedure easier and faster to achieve, while maintaining standards.

These might include tips relating to –

- the physical, manual pressure required to perform an operation;
- the detail which must be included to satisfy criteria;
- the importance of adhering to a sequence of operational steps; and
- the indicators which will signify that steps in a sequence of actions have each been completed correctly.

In short, the things that an experienced operator already knows.

The holistic effect

Combine –

- the recognised "official" detail of how to do something;
- the additional tips and techniques; and
- adapted input aimed at the needs of the particular learner

- and we have the most effective integrated, holistic message.

Thinking in this way reminds the champion that s/he may have to adapt the message for a subsequent individual learner. Remember, the techniques and materials used effectively with one learner won't necessarily work well for another. However, we can't realistically think in terms of creating totally individualised materials for each learner, so the basic message will remain the same. There will be additional, personalised input and reinforcement which the champion will provide, to help each learner over particular hurdles.

Ambitious championing

Try to expand and extend as far as your own "blue sky thinking" nerve will allow.

You may –

- identify elements in some procedure or activity which could be transferred for use in others to good effect;
- have ways of doing things in your life aspect which could be applied effectively at work – with any necessary amendments;
- question why a certain new policy is implemented in a certain way, proposing possible alternatives; and
- feel confident enough to keep questioning why proposed changes are necessary – and probing the detail of these changes.

Entrepreneurial-style thinking is very valuable – if you have it, make best use of it.

Cause and Effect

Holistic thought can meet the light of day in a variety of different shapes and forms. It's more likely to expand and flourish where the foundations of a more open, altruistic life already exist within you – and remain firmly in place.

In simple terms, keep asking yourself –

- "Are there other activities that can be combined with this one which will give a heightened result?"
- "Are there other ways of doing this which would additionally involve others and improve the end result beyond general expectations?"
- "Are there additional activities which I can include, which will make the outcome more positive and beneficial to others as well as myself?"

It's a straight-forward message but the results can be very dramatic.

Holistic conclusions

In the light of our business application considerations, review the following tenets for a more altruistic work/life development plan:

- *Build positive thought.*
- *Be aware of yourself and others.*
- *Believe in yourself and others.*
- *Act as selflessly as you can.*
- *Allow time to do things properly.*

- *Give matters time to evolve.*
- *Allow yourself "Time Out" for thinking.*
- *Rest, relax and apply meditation/mind focus.*
- *Use visualisation to concentrate thought.*
- *Observe and learn from world affairs.*
- *Work towards co-operation and away from egocentricity.*
- *Consider the effects of your actions.*
- *Apply holistic thinking when the time seems appropriate.*
- *Do what ultimately feels right.*
- *Reduce your dependence on stimulants and medication.*
- *Believe in the healing power of positive thought.*
- *Exercise in as natural an environment as possible.*
- *Retain an overview of the Bigger Picture.*
- *Maintain a flexible view of your development path.*
- *Amend your plans openly to maintain progress.*

12 Working with Your Team

One-minute recap and overview

So, here we are, having viewed the complete vista around us. We've: established the integrated approach towards workplace championing; reviewed its roles and criteria in encouraging workplace learning and co-operation; seen how champions and learners can work together to broaden and increase competencies throughout your organisation; and identified how this can lead to a holistic bonus or synergy. It's this group synergy that we shall now be focusing on in greater detail.

Building the team spirit

It's important that team building activities are both relevant to the individuals involved and applicable within the workplace. We have, after all, been consistently underlining the importance of practical involvement directly reinforcing and consolidating the learning. Business communication exercises, for example, can be used as the vehicle for developing team cohesiveness – which will have longer-term applicability than building a raft or handling imaginary drums of radioactive material! The Presentation Planning case study at the end of chapter seven illustrates how individuals can work together co-operatively, with a valuable, usable end result.

Mutual help and assistance: sharing, blending and building

As an extension to this, if we consider our broad-based championing applications holistically, we can see how sharing, blending and building upon competency areas is very likely to help the development of our team synergy. People working as members of a cohesive team will be more inclined to help each other. Additionally, people working within an atmosphere of mutual help and assistance should find it easier to blend together as a team.

Sporting analogies: individuals co-operating in teams

In the motivational speaking circuit, there's a lot made of individuals playing as a member of a football, rugby or cricket team – basically, a rugby team can't function properly without individuals co-operating ... football teams squander goal-scoring opportunities when individual players lose sight of better-placed colleagues. Motivationally however, the longer-term synergy and co-operative interactions required within the business context are harder to maintain than during a sports fixture of finite duration – but lessons can certainly be transferred.

If it has been allowed and assisted to grow, the championing element of our integrated triangle model will have encouraged the growth of "confident competency" which we have mentioned periodically. Pause for a moment and consider the range of benefits which this can bring to your company environment.

Focus Time 12.1

Confident competency creates the situation where:

- *individuals are able to work smarter, at a wider range of tasks;*
- *individuals become more conscious of the special skills of others;*
- *teams build, with added effectiveness through skills sharing;*
- *individuals gain confidence through championing others in key skills;*
- *champions reinforce their own skills through working with others; and*
- *the team works more confidently together, sharing responsibilities.*

Creating this atmosphere – even gradually – and monitoring its development will give us a working environment where co-operative thinking is more likely to evolve consistently. As I have written elsewhere –

"You can reach the mountain top without stepping on the heads of those who follow."

Responding naturally

In fact, mountain climbing is another activity which brings out the best in individuals co-operating with others. No climber or hill walker would walk past another in difficulty without offering assistance. Is it the type of person involved? Perhaps it's the generally understood code of practice in the hills? Or perhaps being exposed to the natural elements makes us more likely to act as we should do – naturally?

Whatever the reasoning, applying this more holistic, altruistic way of thinking in life generally – including business dealings – is likely to make us more confidently competent at interacting in an open and honest way.

Work/life transfers

It remains a source of some puzzlement and disappointment that the more open and honest decisions which are often made on the mountain, sports field or in the family environment without a second thought can be thought of as being weak and non-assertive when applied in the business world. Why should there be one set of "rules of engagement" for our life aspects, with another for work? We are the same people involved in both aspects, after all.

Mountains and Managers

Being realistic, there will always be individuals within the business environment who find it hard to think and act co-operatively. Where they are in senior positions, this can make the holistic team situation harder to develop and maintain. You're more likely to see the tide turning positively when the overall effect can be seen to affect the "bottom line" positively. We can respond to this by selecting our initial projects judiciously.

As suggested previously, we're also more likely to receive support where we carefully select the departments for our initial championing efforts. Selecting departments where managers are positively in favour of our championing ideas makes sense. The results are more likely to be positive – and additional co-operative involvement with new departments will grow as a direct result.

The hundred monkeys' principle

This is the "hundred monkeys' principle" that was mentioned earlier – where a critical mass point must first be achieved, getting that crucial percentage of people thinking in the same way. Reaching this point produces enough people "converted" to the new way of thinking to create a majority. The new acceptable stance will then accelerate. Changes in clothing fashions follow this path (remember flared trousers, which disappear, then reappear every so often?).

The waxing and waning public support for retaining or ejecting "celebrities" in reality TV shows is another clear example. The political change in Spain in 2004, in response to doubts about the government's claims of responsibility for the Madrid bombing was a vivid example of the principle working very rapidly, to immediate effect. Similar thinking continues to dog at the heels of the Iraq situation. It appears in many different guises – with dramatic results when the critical mass point is achieved.

Maintaining progress

The moral therefore is that, if we remain clear in our own minds about the direction of our path along the competency track – and are convinced of the benefits to ourselves and others of taking this path – we are more likely to convince and convert others.

Remember the "7 Cs" which we have mentioned periodically –

- *competency*
- *consistency* and
- *co-operation*

have been key, recurring themes.

Effective two-way *communication* is the solution to many a business problem – or if applied in the early stages of a developing situation, a prevention strategy.

An experienced individual who is *conversant* with the skills and knowledge required – and who displays *creativity* by "thinking outside the box", will display the *credibility* necessary to be a star workplace champion.

Growing the effect: encouraging others to take part

And, where we initially start with a few individuals co-operating with others through workplace championing, their successful outcomes will encourage others to take part. This strategy, of growing towards an overall improvement in competency levels, will gradually bring more and more participants on board, once they see the benefits of involvement. This is real teambuilding – giving a long-term, ever-expanding effect through demonstrable conviction that it's the correct way forward. Once achieved, this conviction can be shaken – but never completely overturned.

Toe by Toe (a mentoring project set up by the Shannon Trust)

A mentoring project called Toe by Toe, was set up by the Shannon Trust in 1996, where literate prisoners mentored others who came to the project illiterate, teaching them to read. The holistic effect of this has proved to be tangible, with increased self-esteem, improved work potential post-prison and a heightened ability to exist and function in a world heavily reliant on reading competency.

If a holistic workplace championing atmosphere can develop positively like this within a prison setting, it can surely be permitted to develop elsewhere. A gradual change in business mindset from short to longer term thinking – and a greater response to stakeholder involvement and outcomes – will help move this development forward, for the good of the vast majority.

Financial profit is of course important for the existence and growth of any business – but so too are the benefits of positive social, moral and emotional development. Where enough individuals seek a greater emotional benefit as both employee and customer, entrepreneurs will spot and respond to the commercial potential. This in turn will reflect on the scope of the work/life balance which evolves. Stress and long working hours are becoming ever-increasing problems, which must ultimately be addressed properly.

The range of involvement possible

As we've established, a championing contract can be agreed between champion and individual learner (with additional support) for virtually any subject. In so doing, we're potentially creating the most appropriate atmosphere to permit the reinforcement of learning and competency achievement to take place within the workplace.

The continuing need for formal training

As we've also established, more formal training will certainly be the preferred method of transferring learning for specific situations. This might apply, for example, where there are groups of parallel-level learners or where a particular detailed process must be followed identically by all. However, even in these more formal training inputs, there can be a marked add-on benefit in providing post-course reinforcement using champions to supervise practical consolidating applications in the workplace.

Range of championing techniques

Because individual learners may each prefer to learn using different techniques, we must be aware of and apply as wide a range of techniques as possible. Get to know each individual learner's preferences – check, if there ever appears to be a learning blockage ... if in doubt, ask. Parallel the situation with how you might feel when trying to learn a particularly difficult subject area, applying a technique which didn't immediately suit. Keep trying to see things from the other person's point of view – this is the essence of good customer service. When you're acting as a workplace champion, the learner is your client. Find out about the different key championing techniques which are possible – we considered some of them in chapter five.

Championing matters

Encouraging the widespread use of workplace championing isn't easy – no-one's pretending it is – and it's inviting additional workload to individuals (including you) who could happily do without it. But if you consider it to be "working SMART" ... expending initial, structured effort to save later remedial response and associated stress ... and it perhaps begins to make sense.

How many of us, when faced with a colleague who doesn't know how to do something and is making a mess of it, take the immediate option of doing it ourselves rather than spending the time to show the colleague how to do it? Sometimes, time pressures mean we have to – but it often pays off to think in the longer term.

Spend a little – save a lot

Pushing the colleague aside (actually or metaphorically) to do the job yourself means that you leave him/her both demoralised and still incapable of doing the job. So, what happens the next time s/he approaches the same task?

S/he either –

- won't bother trying or
- will mess up once more or
- will ask you to do it again

... thereby wasting future time for yourself and others in resolving the problems.

Take the time to work with him/her patiently once more at that point and, progressively, your colleague will become competent to do the job and free you up to do other things. That is essentially the message behind workplace championing.

Action Time 12.1

Think back over the previous two or three working days (or you may prefer to monitor your next few working days closely).

Go through a time mapping exercise of charting the amount of time you spent during each day doing or redoing work which was really the responsibility of others.

Notice if some of your involvement might be because others don't know how to do it properly, have messed up in the past and lost their confidence or because you "find it easier to just do the work yourself".

Review your list – these are the areas which, with a bit of championing, you could delegate to others, freeing you up to do the important things you're really paid to do. Make a list of some of those key activities now.

Championing competency investments

Devoting an hour to working with your colleague now can thus save you (and others) many hours – and much stress – in the future. Equally, the situation where you receive some input from someone else, at some other time, when **you** require championing, will make **you** more confidently competent – and capable of doing that new task on your own. Think of these inputs as "competency investments" – little bursts of activity ... visualised as the tiny flashes of energy on our meandering paths along the development track. These will inspire trust and save time overall, if we can only think "bigger picture".

The holistic view of the life/work balance

In summary, this involvement is all part of taking a more holistic view of life and work. Encouragingly, we increasingly hear these terms "holistic" and "big picture thinking" being used in conventional contexts. Holistically, workplace championing fits in to become part of the overall CPD (continuing professional development) plan, alongside formal training, general involvement and experience. And, of course, if you act as a champion for a colleague, this activity can be included as part of your personal development (as imparter of new information) in parallel with the professional development received by your learner/colleague. Every little counts.

Training department becomes development support

Think of our workplace championing as an integral part of the overall development process. Appreciate, especially in the early stages, the blocks and difficulties which the training department might have in accepting the new concept. Work with them towards gradually seeing it as an opportunity rather than a threat.

It would doubtless have been preferable if they'd been totally on board before you were involved. It's probably fair to assume, however, that some of the realities and responsibilities will only become totally apparent when the overall championing programme is up and running. Remember the hundred monkeys' principle. Stick with it through these developing times – it's worth it!

Holistic add-on benefits

Holistic thinking is broad based thinking. In a parallel world, there's a lot of talk about "sustainable building" at the moment. Some see this as being largely the use of natural materials to create an environmentally friendly space. This is certainly a strong element but "sustainability" also involves the building being long-lasting, maintainable by those responsible, as well as meeting (and supporting) the additional social, environmental, developmental and health needs of the owners.

It is this "add-on extra" growth potential which is the wonderful bonus of the holistic approach. A similar bonus effect is gained with human interactions as well.

Business in the community

The holistic approach can be equally apparent – and valuable – in the business world. But it needs an open approach. As the late Dame Anita Roddick said in her keynote address to the 2004 CIPD Scottish Conference – "It's a myth that business's sole function is to make money. We need business to safeguard communities, the environment and families." The wide-scale application of workplace championing can engender this growing atmosphere of mutual help, support and co-operation within any organisation or community.

Applying it holistically throughout a business community can provide a key driving force for broadening the attitudes which businesses have towards their staff. Once started, the momentum must be maintained positively and long-term. It only needs one negative put-down to undermine the enthusiasm and throw a major blockage across the track. The efforts required to overcome this negativity would in all cases have been better spent encouraging forward progress of individual paths.

Using the integrated triangle model positively

Remember the elastic band round the fingers – remember the dynamic flexibility or synergy which we have established as being a very important component of the model.

Championing within context

This book focuses very strongly on the championing corner of the integrated triangle – details of the supporting titles and model follow in the appendix. But, as the elastic band, synergy exercise illustrated, each corner of the triangle affects the others, so we can't consider workplace championing in isolation. Remember that once the process is fully operational, everyone, including you, is likely to wear both champion and individual learner hats, in different phases of developing continuing professional development (CPD) activities. See it from both aspects and your objectivity and awareness will evolve naturally.

The champion and development support (DSF)

Consider also the champion's role in encouraging the development support function corner of the triangular model. OK – you might see it as HR/training's responsibility to do all the driving forward. You are, after all, agreeing to become involved in elements of training and development which may not traditionally have been seen as your responsibility within the company. That's true – and they should be positively aware (and appreciative) of these extra efforts which you're making.

As a piece of basic inter-personal involvement, however, the atmosphere of your relationship will improve greatly if you –

- allow as much prior warning of any requirements as possible;
- check on progress rather than leaving it to the last minute;
- explain these requirements in as much detail as possible;
- show an awareness of the development time involved;
- discuss any particular problems you have, honestly and openly; and
- keep an eye on progress and reinforce requests if necessary.

Coping with increasing popularity

As more and more people become actively involved in the workplace championing strategy, it'll become increasingly difficult for the support function to respond to the expanding range of specific requirements. However, with the budget released through fewer public course placements, the function can invest in building a bank of resources (sourced both commercially and by internal production). This will provide a degree of rapid championing response for particular needs, as the supporting resource bank gradually broadens.

The scope of champions: building a dynamic team of subject specialists

With positive results through structured responses, the support function will realise the fantastic scope that a championing strategy can bring to their company's development programme. As this appreciation grows, the DSF should be doing everything available within their time constraints to foster relationships. The scope for building a dynamic team of subject specialists available to coach, mentor and informally train others is vast. Integrating these into the company's overall staff development strategy will dramatically increase the potential to respond rapidly to wide-ranging learning needs.

Conducive atmosphere – widespread involvement

Building a positive climate such as this will certainly help the strategy grow. Throughout this book, we have been considering examples of techniques and methods which can be applied towards fostering this atmosphere. We've underlined that efforts must be consistently made by all members of the triangle (individual learner, champion and support function) to maintain positive progress.

As workplace champion, you certainly cannot respond instantly to any and every request. You have your own job to do and these coaching and mentoring activities must slot comfortably within your day-to-day responsibilities.

But sometimes, you'll be required to differentiate between –

- a championing need which is a quick five minute injection to get someone moving again – and
- other occasions which require a more detailed, planned response, extending over a longer period of time to include consolidation.

Rapid response to short requests

You've probably been in the position of sitting in front of your computer screen, not knowing how to access a particular process – a blockage which a quick demonstration from a colleague can overturn, making you productive again. If workplace champions (and others) can respond rapidly to these particular short requests, think of the improved overall efficiency that can result.

Honest open-ness: not being afraid to ask

Think also – if there's a general atmosphere where individuals are no longer afraid to ask for assistance from each other, any atmosphere of personal point scoring which might have existed will diminish. It's no longer an admission of failure or (in extreme cases) potential exposure to ridicule.

When the hundred monkeys' principle kicks in, those continuing to act in a negatively assertive manner will stand out as the disruptive agitators that they really are. Then the majority can isolate them – never forget, you can be both honest and assertive, on your path towards co-operation!

Remaining doubts

In this final chapter, we've been extolling the benefits of initiating a workplace championing approach within your company. In any decision making activity, there will always be remaining doubts – and perhaps queries which require further response. When attempting to get the strategy off the ground, within the context of the integrated triangle model, there will undoubtedly be false dawns and occasions where heads appear to be beating firmly against brick walls. To maintain your motivation when the energy glow is flickering somewhat, remember to –

- start small;
- seek out fellow enthusiasts for a pilot programme;
- select a simple subject area – likely to have a strong impact;
- canvas support from senior management at the planning stage;
- create a short programme, to allow outcomes to be noticed soon;
- work closely with the support function – responding to their advice;
- publicise the progress and success of the programme; and
- encourage departments to request help for new programmes.

Get these simple strategies right and you'll be more likely to build steadily on your firm foundations. Photocopy this memo list and stick it on your wall, if that helps!

Senior management support

Talk to the right people – get your senior managers on-side and being supportive. They should be directly involved but, at the very least, they must be **seen** to be supporting the initiative.

This can be by simple signs like –

- showing a positive attitude towards the release of staff;
- supporting the access to resources; and
- encouraging the HR/training department (our DSF) to play an active part, through board-level policy decisions.

Crucially, this support must be both consistent and long-term.

Sure – this is easier said than done – it's part of encouraging the "putting of management money where mouths are". However, it's not enough to mouth the mission statement-type platitudes when it suits – the initiative must be supported consistently, even when priorities are under threat. Great people really are a company's most important asset – a holistic development approach will encourage this great to become brilliant.

Focus on yourself

You're a potential workplace champion. Within the development picture of things, you're also a potential learner. The scope for your continuing professional development (CPD) is huge, if you can encourage the momentum to build. Visualise the development track – and your path along it. On this path, having a clear idea of your personal milestones along the way will give clear indications of your unique championing needs.

Holistic interactions

On occasion, you'll need to include necessary amendments, in order to keep your revised development in line with future change. Quick championing injections of necessary information will allow you to respond to these revisions. Think holistically about the adjacent paths – your colleagues – and the holistic effects of their activities upon each other. This is the synergy which we've been describing consistently as one of the key goals of our integrated model. Visualise – see it grow!

We have lift-off!

Given support and positive thought, this growth will happen. In chapter eight, we reviewed the analogy of flying kites, in order to gain the idea of responding to a variety of ideas simultaneously – and maintaining progress throughout. The integrated triangle is a simple model, based on straight-forward expectations. It requires a co-operative approach towards business dealings, as well as an informed awareness of the best practices for personal interactions. It also requires a "bigger picture" overview of the range of options and opportunities open, in order to keep the range of ideas moving positively upwards.

The next stage

Setting up an integrated championing approach requires time and a fair degree of knowledge and competency. It incorporates an awareness of both formal and informal learning techniques and philosophies with practical experience of change and project management. The very important planning and attitudinal change stages are not easy – but are crucially important. Contact my consultancy company (see appendix) if you require assistance to succeed in implementing the model.

Bringing the Integrated Triangle to Life!

The holistic way forward is certainly a positive step along the track. The surer you are about those first milestones and your path stretching forward between them, the more positively you will move along and the more confidently you can co-operate with others. Do so and experience the buzz of a growing confident competence. It's the holistic route to workplace learning – bringing the Integrated Triangle to Life!

One or two final thoughts to ponder, from – "Messages from the Mountains":

- Administration exists to support – not control.
- Hidden agendas deserve exposure.
- Group co-operation can overcome individual assertion.
- It's always the person above who is creating the problems.
- Lack of awareness is no excuse.
- If you don't apply it, it wasn't worth learning.
- There's got to be more to work than happy shareholders.
- A brief word of praise has a long echo.
- Do it once more and really become the expert.

It's time to start growing!

Appendix

The Integrated Triangle Approach

This book has referred to the Integrated Triangle, and the three elements of which it's composed. These are –

- The Workplace Champion
- The Individual Learner
- The Development Support Function (DSF)

As the title indicates, we've been concentrating on the development of workplace champions – but this has included some consideration of the roles represented by the other two corners of the triangle.

Details of the complete model and its function are set out in a dedicated website – www.the-integrated-triangle.com with each corner represented by a book by the author, concentrating on that particular role and its integration.

Workplace Champion – **Growing Workplace Champions**	Studymates Professional
Individual Learner – **Brilliant Future**	Prentice Hall
DSF – **Planning & Organising Personal & Professional Development**	Gower

A further supporting book – **Freeing the Champion Within** – which is a full length case study examining the growth and development of holistic thinking, covering both life and work aspects, is scheduled for publishing soon.

The inspirational sayings in the final chapter are extracted from two-book set of inspirational saying and poetry by Chris – **Messages from the Mountains and Echoes in the Atrium** – published in late 2006.

The author's consultancy – Chris Sangster Development – is available to work with companies to implement workplace championing strategies within the integrated triangle model – contact Chris on – chris.sangster@btinternet.com

Chris also facilitates a programme of short workshops reinforcing related areas –

The Holistic Route to Workplace Development

- ***Communicating towards Co-operation***
- ***Becoming a Workplace Champion***
- ***Stressing the Positive***
- ***Introducing the Integrated Triangle***

See the website for details of these – and arrangements for discussing customised course provision www.the-integrated-triangle.com

Chris is also available for public speaking engagements on the subject of integrated championing and its various applications – as well as on the subject of downshifting, with reference to the book written jointly with his wife:

The Downshifter's Guide to Relocation HowtoBooks

Chris Sangster Development

contact - chris.sangster@btinternet.com

Index